Come and Sleep
The Folklore of the Japanese Fox

Christopher Kincaid

First Printing, 2015

ISBN: 1532847351
ISBN-13: 978-1532847356

Printed in the United States of America

Table of Contents

Introduction
The Immigrant Fox

Something about the fox—her red fur, her white-tufted tail, or her uncanny intelligence—haunts our history. Our stories speak about the fox more than any other animal.[1] Stories from across the world speak of her as a trickster, a demon, a devoted mother, an ideal wife, and a divine messenger. In Jewish tradition, Samson tied three-hundred foxes together by their tails, fastened torches to them, and let them loose to burn the fields, groves, and vineyards of the Philistines.[2] Europe's tricky fox, Reynard, loves to tweak the noses of medieval aristocrats and clergy. Wherever foxes run, people whisper of their cunning, pranks, and magic. Yet of all cultures that speak of foxes, Japanese culture has a unique relationship with the animal. The vixen wraps her tail around every aspect of Japanese culture, from the thousands of shrines dedicated to Inari, the Shinto Goddess of Rice, to how people answer telephones.

In order to understand Japan, we must first understand the fox. She is a creature of field and farm, and she runs with the common people more than high priests and aristocrats. But this doesn't stop her from playing pranks and causing problems among the ruling class, as even the Shogun Hideyoshi discovered.

The Japanese fox lives on the border of the commonplace and the mysterious, never quite fitting into a neat compartment. The fox tangles positive with negative and divinity with demon. She hunts fields and wanders towns, straddling both the human world and the animal world. Living on this edge gives her the ability to tap into both worlds. Her flexibility in folklore makes her hard to pin down. She is both saint and devil. She represents Japan's soul and humanity's darker drives.

The Origin of Fox Tales

Many scholars believe that Japanese fox stories originated in China around 333 BC and traveled to Japan with other Chinese ideas.[3] Not all scholars agree with this assessment, however. The Ainu, a people native to northern Japan, have their own tradition of fox stories which developed apart from Chinese stories. Japanese fox tales developed features neither Ainu nor Chinese stories have: Inari-foxes and fox-sorcery. The origin of the fox doesn't have to be an either-or scenario. Chinese fox tales can easily mix with Ainu and other native stories to create the Japanese vixen. One fox story captures the relationship of Japanese fox tales to their origin stories from China:

One day all the animals in Japan heard the tiger, king of beasts, was coming to their country to fight with them. They were afraid that the tiger would prove too powerful for the bear, so the fox was ordered to meet the tiger, and if possible outwit him with cunning; failing that, the bear would try his strength. The tiger, having reached Japan, came to a large forest a thousand miles in diameter. The fox met him and said, "How do you do, sir? I have heard you are the king of animals in foreign countries. Is it true, great sir?"

"Yes, I am, and no one can run faster than me."

"Then will you not run a race with me?" asked the fox.

"Yes, but you don't suppose you can win, do you?" said the tiger.

They retired to one side of the forest and began to run. The cunning fox lightly leaped up and laid hold of the tiger's tail. The tiger, intent on the race, ran until exhausted. The sly fox leapt over his head and was declared the winner.[4]

This story refers to the conflict between China, the tiger, and Japan, the fox. But the tale reveals how the fox rode into Japan on the tail of China's influence. Native and imported fox stories ran the breadth of Japan on the fast moving influence of Chinese culture. On their journey, the tales became something unique to Japanese culture, building and expanding upon the patterns China provided.

The story also points to the cunning of the Japanese fox. She understands she couldn't fight the tiger like the bear could. In fact, the animals worry the bear lacks the tiger's strength. So they ask the fox to use her cunning to outwit the tiger. In another Chinese fable from 333 BC, the fox warns the tiger to beware her cunning:

> The Sovereign of Heaven has privileged me among all animals by giving me greater cunning than to others. Should you devour me, you would certainly displease him very much. [5]

Fox Behavior and Traits

Understanding basic fox behavior helps us understand why the fox tickles our imagination. Despite being a canine, the fox shares more in common with cats than with dogs. She stalks prey like a cat does, and she has paws with partially retractable claws. She even has vertical-slit pupils like a cat.

Foxes dash across the northern hemisphere and live in a variety of environments. Afghanistan, Pakistan, and Iran have desert foxes. The Arctic Circle has its own type of fox. The fox lives and adapts to its environment with ease because she can eat a variety of food. A study in Missouri found foxes eat 34 different mammals, 14 species of birds, 15 families of insects, and 21 varieties of plants.[6] They change their diet based on the season and climate. During summer and autumn, foxes often eat berries and fruit and bury surplus food to eat later. When burying food in snow, the fox will disguise the cache and brush away her paw prints.[7] Not only does this behavior suggest forethought, but it also reveals foxes' intelligence and cunning. In fact, foxes can remember dozens of cache locations.

Foxes are solitary hunters, but they also form monogamous relationships to raise kits. Unlike many animals, both male and female foxes care for their young, and daughters from previous litters sometimes help with raising their siblings.[8] Fox families provide a foundation for folktales about human-fox relationships and the idea of the divine-mother fox. Folktales do not come out of mere superstition. The stories enhance what people understand and try to explain the mysteries they can not.

The Folklore Fox's Traits and Abilities

Based on their observations of living foxes, Chinese, Japanese, and Ainu stories agree: some foxes are good, and others are evil. Luckily, we can know a fox by its color. The Japanese red fox's fur can change to white during winter months. Black-furred foxes hunt across Japan and China. The black fox and the white fox bring good luck.[9] The common red fox brings trouble, but she can change into a good fox with time and religious training. Chinese stories clear up this complication by creating two classes of foxes. Celestial foxes, considered good foxes, have white or black fur and a set of nine tails. These foxes were originally red foxes that lived for 1,000 years and became wise with their age. Japanese stories associate the nine-tailed white fox with the goddess Inari.[10] The other category includes the troublemakers: the wild foxes. Folktales love these foxes. They play pranks and bewitch people. They possess people and shave the heads of unwary travelers, but not all wild foxes cause trouble. The category includes many good-hearted foxes destined to become celestial foxes and divine-mothers.

Chinese wild fox stories provide most of the traits characteristic to the Japanese fox. She shape-shifts, bewitches, and possesses. According to both Ainu and Chinese stories, the fox can turn into anything, including a teakettle. Her shape-shifting antics often go awry. As you can imagine, turning into a teakettle isn't the brightest idea. In another story, a fox changed into a tree with a similar unhappy result:

> Nakadayu, the nephew to the chief Shinto priest of the Kasuga shrine at Nara, was once roaming about with his servant towards evening

in a lonely mountain when they spied a gigantic cedar tree standing ahead of them, about 200 feet high.

Said Nakadayu to his servant:

"I never saw such a big cedar tree standing near here on this mountain before. Can you see the tree yonder?"

"Yes, master," answered the servant, "I can see a big cedar tree over there."

"I don't think we have such a gigantic cedar tree even in other parts of this province," said Nakadayu.

"We have cedar trees in this province. However I have never seen such a big one before," agreed the servant.

"In that case," observed Nakadayu, "we might have been bewitched by a fox. We had better go home now."

They had been walking about the mountain to cut plenty of grass for the horse kept at Nakadayu's house. They were unaware of the passing of time. In the gathering dusk, they saw the moon rise and cast a weird light on the cedar tree. A nocturnal bird screeched somewhere. A bush nearby rustled in the stillness of the mountain as if a bandit lurking behind it were coming out.

Master and servant exchanged glances, and each of them fixed an arrow to the string of the bow they were carrying for self-defense. A squirrel appeared and quickly vanished across the path.

"Before we go home," said the servant, "let us shoot the cedar tree and come here again tomorrow morning to see it."

They notched an arrow upon their bows.

"We had better shoot the cedar tree from a shorter distance," advised the servant.

The proceeded a little farther—drew their bows to their full extent—and both shot the giant tree at the same time.

"Whiz!" went the arrows—and the next moment they saw the huge tree disappear!

They were afraid that it might be the act of some uncanny hand, so they left the spot without delay.

The following morning they found an old fox shot dead by two arrows stuck in its body at the very spot where the gigantic cedar tree had been observed standing by Nakadayu and his servant.

The prank of the fox cost it its life.[11]

When I first read this story, I had to ask myself: why would a fox turn into a tree? It is a rather boring prank. But when you think about it, many people use landmarks to navigate through forests. A large cedar tree makes a good landmark. By shape-shifting into such a tree and then moving around, the fox could trick anyone who is using the tree as a landmark. The victim could well become lost, much to the fox's delight. Only this time, the fox's trick turns against it. Nakadayu and his servant know the woods well enough to suspect the tree is a fox. This suggests the fox was known to play such tricks.

While the fox can change into objects far larger than her real size, she prefers to transform into a human woman. As a fox ages, she transforms into increasingly beautiful women, and the 1,000-year-old fox transforms into the loveliest of all women. Her experience with human society allows her to better judge human ideals of beauty. Age also lends practice. Old foxes do not need illusion to complete a disguise, unlike young foxes. Young foxes keep their shape-change and illusion only long enough to finish their tricks.

You may notice how I refer to the fox as female. For the Japanese, the fox is foremost a woman. Male foxes appear rarely in Japanese tales. The Japanese vixen uses her beauty and shape-shifting ability to conjure illusions in order to bewitch people.

Her illusions can turn graves into large houses, as one traveling singer discovered:

In the An-ei era. (1772-1780) a well-known *joruri*-actor [*joruri* singing a story to the sound of a *shamisen*] was richly entertained in a large farmer's house, where a big crowd filled the room and enthusiastically applauded him when he gave proof of his talent. After he had recited a long time, suddenly it became silent about him and lo! he was alone. No house, no room was to be seen, and in the dim morning light he found himself in a graveyard! Hastily he fled away home in the belief that foxes had deceived him and given him horse dung and cow urine instead of nice food and wine. The idea made him ill and confused, and for some days he kept to his bed.

In the meantime, the rumor rapidly spread all over the province that he had been haunted by foxes which had asked him to play for them. And this was true; but his suspicion about the food and wine the brutes had offered him was not correct, for on that same night a wedding had taken place in a neighboring village, and all the eatables and drinkables which were ready for the guests had disappeared in a mysterious way. That was certainly the work of foxes or *tanuki*, for on the moor where they had entertained the actor, fish-bones, and wine- cups lay spread about. Apparently, the foxes, admiring his art, had offered him the food and wine stolen from the wedding party. After some days the actor recovered, but he henceforth chose another profession and only recited *joruri* now and then at somebody's request.[12]

Fox spirits share illusion magic with their physical sisters, but the spirit forms can possess people to create more powerful illusions. Possession allows the fox spirit to take control of the victim and directly shape the victim's perception of reality. The belief in possession and bewitching foxes has remained surprisingly stubborn. Westernization during the Meiji Reformation did little to quell the beliefs. Even as recent as 1983, a woman was diagnosed as being possessed by a fox.[13]

Beyond using her powers on people, the fox's presence impacts people on a social level.

Japan inherited the idea of fox-ownership from China. Fox-ownership occurs when a fox spirit decides to adopt a hapless family. The family prospers under the patronage of the fox but at the expense of the family's neighbors. The fox spirit possesses and pranks the family's rivals and steals wealth to give to her adopted humans. This hurts the adopted family's reputation, and the village blames the family for any theft that happens. Because of this phenomenon, people who owned a fox were banned from the community. Fox-ownership even caused a lover's suicide as recently as 1953.[14] Families inherited fox spirits and passed the spirit on through marriage. Because of this, being labeled as a fox-owner became a part of the family's identity, and few in the local community wanted to marry into such a negative label.

Not all traits of the Japanese fox came from China. Two unique traits developed in Japan. Strangely, these traits failed to travel back to China. As I mentioned earlier, the fox and the popular idea of the goddess Inari are inseparable. Both Chinese and Ainu fox stories lack any sort of fox deity. As the goddess of rice and wealth, Inari and her shrines scatter throughout Japan. Foxes often visit these shrines in their search for food. A natural relationship developed out of this. The fox's close association with the goddess combines with the Chinese category of divine foxes to create a hierarchy. Inari foxes are good, divine foxes charged with punishing their wild cousins. One tale shows Inari foxes punishing a wild fox for eating a turtle at a temple. A visiting lord heard of the desecration and ordered a hunt for the fox.

> That night he heard some noises in front
> of his room, and when he opened the door and
> looked out, he saw a fox, bound with creeping
> vines, the ends of which two other foxes held in
> their mouths. Upon the Lord's question as to what

they intended to do with the culprit, they attacked
the animal and killed it at once.[15]

The other trait unique to Japanese fox lore is fox-sorcery. Fox-sorcerers use a fox as the source of their magic, much like the black cat of a witch. In addition to gaining a fox that can cast illusions and shape-shift, the sorcerer gains the fox's divination and possession abilities.

The Japanese fox barks a complex story. Let's run with her and learn about her life, starting with her role as the ideal wife and as a shape-shifting prankster. As we chase her through the forest and city streets, we will hear the tales people share about her.

Fox tales reveal truths about human behavior and Japanese culture. Stories of affectionate vixens touch on the tragedy of love and unavoidable loss we must all face when a loved one dies. Stories of the fox's gratitude suggest how we too should be grateful for life and kindness. Fox-ownership reveals ugly truths about how communities treat those viewed as different or threatening. In all of these ways, the fox embodies Japanese ideals and fears. In the form of a woman—ideal wife and divine mother—she represents the soul of Japan.

Chapter 1
The Shifty, Sexy Fox

She moves like a willow caressed by the wind. Her skin, whiter than a freshly painted *geisha*, defies the sun's labors. After all, only vulgar leather farmwives tan. She purses her cherry-blossom lips and adjusts her hairpins. Sunlight kisses her arranged black hair. Blue hints shimmer. Her small, aristocratic nose and her liquid eyes—angled just so—grace a face marred by being a touch too long. But somehow even that defect completes the perfection of her beauty. She watches you, her gaze measuring, considering, and veiling.

The fox stalks the shrew.

The oldest fox stories found in China and Japan speak about alluring and mysterious fox women. Chinese vixen tales portray female foxes as erotic, dangerous, and even vampiric creatures. Only a small number of these Chinese shape-shifting stories carry a positive view of the fox, and these tales all end with the fox's death.[16] Unlike the Japanese fox, Chinese foxes work toward a goal: to become an immortal human. She will do anything to achieve humanity and immortality, but most often she uses sex to gather men's *yang*. A fragment of a Chinese tale gives us an example:

Wu Lintang also told of a young man who was seduced by a fox, and though he was gradually wasting away, the fox kept coming. His energies became so depleted that finally, he was not able to satisfy her when the two were in bed together. Putting on her clothes, the fox made ready to depart. Much as the young man, weeping, implored her to stay, she adamantly refused.

When reprimanded for her lack of feelings, the fox retorted in anger, "There are no marital obligations between us; I came for the specific purpose of getting spiritual nourishment. The cream and essence of your being have been exhausted. With nothing more to gain, why should I not go? This is like liaisons built on power and influence that are broken when there is no more power or influence. Liaisons built on wealth, too, are severed when there is no more wealth. Humans carry favor with those whose wealth and power have aroused their attention, not out of any genuine feelings. Previously didn't you ingratiate yourself with so-and-so, whom you now no longer care about? And I am being reproached!"[17]

The concept of *yin-yang* describes two complimenting energies found in living creatures. Most people know the classic symbol of a half-black (*yin*) and half white (*yang*) disk cut by a sinuous line. Both halves contain a circle of the opposite force, and the outer circle completes when *yin* and *yang* join. Female Chinese foxes possess the *yin* aspect and need *yang* to reach their goal. In order to balance themselves, they harvest male *yang* by having sex. During the Ming dynasty, having sex with a fox resulted in a long life for the man. However, during the Qing dynasty, foxes transformed into women to drain men of their vital energy, eventually killing them.[18] In some Chinese folktales, male foxes love hanging around women's bedrooms and waiting for a woman to have her period. They relish licking the discarded rags soaked in menstrual blood in order to balance their *yang*.

Contrary to the Japanese view of the fox as a woman, most Chinese stories focus on male foxes. Male fox spirits lavish their attention on women and bring wealth to the family. These fox spirits steal from others in the village and use the wealth to seduce wives. Poor families regularly sold or rented wives, daughters, and daughter-in-laws. For many families, the bodies of women were the last means for survival during the late imperial period of China.[19] The idea of a male fox offering money in return for enjoying a wife's charms made this desperate practice a little more acceptable. After all, the fox was a spirit-being instead of a typical prostitute's client. At least, the story sounds better than telling a nosy neighbor what was really happening. Folk stories allowed people to justify a desperate decision by providing a precedent.

Japan inherited these stories and much more. Despite the rarity of Chinese female-fox stories, they resonated with the Japanese more than male fox stories. The idea of a male fox seducing wives gained some traction, but even in these cases, most foxes were considered female. Instead of using seduction, these foxes possessed wives. The change of emphasis came from the tight rules Japanese society used to regulate prostitution. People didn't need fox stories to justify what was a state-regulated practice.

The Jewel Maiden

In any case, Chinese fox stories passed to Japan along with Confucianism and other Chinese cultural exports. The most influential female-fox story Japan imported was "The Jewel Maiden." The Japanese telling adds a redemptive twist on this primarily negative female-fox tale. The redemptive ending reflects the unique Japanese view of the beautiful fox as mostly a positive and tragic figure.

"The Jewel Maiden" marks the decline of imperial power at the end of the Heian period in Japan.[20] The end of the Heian period (794-1185 AD) causes the Japanese emperor to lose some of his authority to the warrior class, who would later become the samurai. "The Jewel Maiden" immigrates during this time of upheaval. In the original Chinese story, the emperor falls for a mysterious woman named Daji who turns out to be a nine-tailed fox. This affair ultimately leads to the destruction of the Shang line of emperors. According to the story, Daji introduces the Chinese practice foot-binding to keep women's feet abnormally small.[21] The Japanese version follows the same pattern as Daji's story (without the foot-binding practice), but it adds a redemptive ending for the nine-tailed kingdom destroyer. In the Chinese story, a magic mirror destroys her.

I will paraphrase the story, but if you want to read a full version, you can find a selection in Further Reading section.

During the reign of the retired emperor Toba-no-in, who rules Japan behind the scenes, a mysterious woman appears at the court. She lacks the proper family connections, but her beauty and education stand beyond the reach of any other court lady. She quickly becomes the retired emperor's favorite and rarely leaves his side. One night, a fierce storm shakes the palace, and the court tries to distract themselves with an evening of music and poetry. Suddenly, the wind bursts into the room and extinguishes all the lamps. Only the darkness is not total. A soft glow cuts the night, radiating from the emperor's mistress. This terrifies everyone in the court, except Toba. He sees it as a sign that his favorite lady transcended normal spirituality and names her *Tamamo no mae,* the Jewel Maiden.

Soon after the event, the retired emperor and his son, the reigning emperor Konoe, fall ill. The court exorcist, Abe no Yasunari, suspects foul play on the part of the Jewel Maiden after her glowing incident. Abe decides to reveal the truth about the woman. Insisting the Jewel Maiden take part in a ceremony, Abe uses the ritual as a cover for his exorcism incantations.

As he finishes his last incantation, the Jewel Maiden, writhing with pain, transforms into her true form: a nine-tailed fox. She flies off, and Abe orders two of the court's best warriors to put an end to her. Over several additional adventures, the warriors manage to slay the fox. In the last act of vengeance, the fox transforms her spirit into a stone that spews out poisonous gas that kills everything nearby. The emperor and his son still die despite the efforts of the warriors.

Around a century later, the Zen practitioner Genyo travels to the stone to put an end to its killing. Because his immense spiritual powers protect him from the deadly fumes, Genyo saunters right up to the stone without any problems. The spirit of the fox, sensing her end, confesses to him all that she did. In India, she convinces the king to invade his neighbors and use the prisoners for a bloody ritual. She speaks of her time in China and of the end of its dynasty. Finally, she tells the story of Toba. In response to her stories, Genyo hits the stone with his staff—cleaving it in half—and teaches her the errors of her life. After hearing his teaching, the Jewel Maiden's spirit lifts from the stone and ascends to a positive rebirth with other celestial beings and nine-tailed foxes.

Considering the original, negative Chinese view of Daji, the retelling's ending suggests how Japanese folklore regards female foxes as generally positive. Even a fox that brought down rulers in the three kingdoms of India, China, and Japan can be redeemed. The story also showcases the power of Zen Buddhism. It takes a Zen practitioner to end the terror of the fox. While the "Jewel Maiden" is the most important fox story Japan inherits from China—inspiring a popular *noh* drama—it is still not the *most* important fox tale. That honor belongs to the fox-wife story "On Taking a Fox as a Wife and Bringing Forth a Child." This story is the oldest and creates the template for all other fox-wife tales that follow. Its first appearance in literature dates to the 9th century, and the story tells of how the Japanese fox gained her name.[22] But before we can dive into "On Taking a Fox as a Wife and Bringing Forth a Child," we first need to dig a little deeper into the attitudes toward women at the time. Understanding these attitudes will help us understand the importance of these fox-wife tales.

Attitudes toward Women

Nonhuman wife stories can only be found in Japan and surrounding areas.[23] Marriage between people and animals doesn't happen in Western tales.[24] Considering the social attitudes toward women when fox-wife stories became popular, the tales are even more remarkable. Feudal China and Japan shared a negative view of women. This view varied depending on the time period. For example, a man having sex with female foxes during the Ming dynasty granted him a long life. This was a fairly positive outlook on fox-women despite being still male-oriented. However, during the Qing dynasty, the same foxes fed off the man's life force. There were exceptions. For example, some Qing fox stories included good foxes as lovers. Male foxes also took on the important duty of guarding official seals and documents.[25] Generalizations can mislead, but there was a firmly negative view of women in Japanese society just as fox-tales developed. A study of Japanese proverbs by Hiroko Storm provides some insight.

In the study, Storm classified Japanese proverbs dealing with women. Not all of these proverbs date from the same period as our seminal fox story. However, Storm's study provides useful insight into the overall view of women throughout Japanese history. Like amber preserves an insect, proverbs bottle ideas from distant periods. They shelter a culture's concerns and wisdom. They fossilize bias. Of the 817 proverbs about women Storm reviews, only 29 were positive. Over 300 are negative, and the rest fall into neutral and neutral-negative ratings. The collection generalizes women as inferior, stupid, ill-natured, weak, and overly talkative. However, the proverbs also reveal a difference between social classes of women. The lower classes, like farmers and merchants, viewed women as important work help. Upper-class women had less importance compared to farm wives.[26] Upper classes didn't need women to help in the fields or lug goods. Their value depended upon childrearing and maintaining the household. Lower-class women shared these responsibilities in addition to their other work. Here are few proverbs Storm quotes to give you an idea of how women were viewed:

> "A smart woman ruins the castle."
> "Women's wisdom is born of greed."
> "Women talk about things senselessly."
> "Frailty, thy name is woman."

The *Tale of Genji* (from the 11th century) sums society's attitude toward women: "If they were not fundamentally evil, they would not have been born women at all." Despite these attitudes, fox-wife stories portray women as ideal helpers and mates. Considering how the fox originates with the farming and merchant classes, this makes sense. Fox-wife tales center on the social role of the wife and mother and how the fox cannot fill that role. Her animal cunning takes her only so far, yet for all her shortfalls the Japanese regard her as an ideal mother and wife. The stories lend hope to women who struggle with the duties of work, running the household, and motherhood. Like the fox, she doesn't have to be perfect to be the ideal wife and mother. Fox-wife stories undermined social norms. The educated fox-wife wields considerable power over the family. In contrast, women had little legal power. During the Tokugawa Shogunate (1602-1868) women didn't legally exist.

They could not own property and had to be subordinate to men.[27]

This environment explains the popularity of the fox-wife tale. For men, the stories show a capable, exotic, and beautiful wife. For women, the stories ink a dutiful and intelligent woman. The fox-wife lifts some of the burdens society placed on men through her intelligence and hard work. The stories allow women to feel empowered in their social role, but the stories do not try to break women out of that role. From our modern perspective, this looks like a failure. After all, they reinforce the idea that a woman's place is in the home. But the stories subvert the negative view of women. The fox-wife shows how an intelligent woman benefits the castle instead of ruining it.

She shows how wisdom comes from love and generosity rather than greed. She speaks with sense and disproves the idea of female frailty.

How the Fox Became Kitsune

Now that we have sketched the stage, let's visit the first fox-wife tale and learn how the Japanese fox gained her name: *Kitsune*.

This took place long ago in the reign of Emperor Kinmei. A man of the Ono district of Mino province set out on his horse in search of a good wife. At that time in a broad field, he came on an attractive woman, who responded to him.

He winked at her and asked, "Where are you going, pretty miss?" She answered, "I am looking for a good husband." "Will you be my wife?" he then asked. She replied, "I will." So he took her home, and they married and lived together.

After a time, on the fifteenth day of the Twelfth Month, their dog gave birth to a puppy. The puppy constantly barked at the wife and threatened to bite her.

She became so frightened that she asked her husband to kill the puppy. But in spite of her request, he would not do so.

Around the Second or Third Month, when the annual quota of rice was being hulled, the wife went to where the female servants were pounding rice to give them some refreshment. The puppy ran after her, trying to bite her. Startled and frightened, she changed into a fox and jumped on top of a hedge. The husband, seeing this, said, "You and I have together produced a child. Therefore, I can never forget you. Whenever I call, come and sleep with me." Thus, following the husband's word she came and slept with him.

At that time his wife, wearing a red dyed skirt, moved slowly and gracefully, trailing her skirt as she went.

The husband, gazing at her figure, sang a love song that went

Love fills me
Completely
But after one moment,
A fleeting gem,
That one—she's gone!

Therefore, they named the child who they had produced Kitsune, which became his surname: Kitsune no atai. The child was famous for his great strength and could run as a bird flies. He is the ancestor of the Kitsune-no-atai family of Mino province.[28]

The word *kitsune* (pronounced *key-tzoon-nay*) means "fox" and "come and sleep." The word derives from the onomatopoeia of the fox's cry.[29] Unlike Chinese stories, the Japanese fox isn't motivated by the selfish quest for immortality. Love motivates her. A revealed fox cannot live in the human world regardless of how much her husband and children love her. She leaves to protect both her own life and the social life of her family. Why does she need to do this to protect them? Because being associated with a

fox creates a stigma toward the family, barring them from partici-
pating in social life. We will look deeper at this idea, called fox-
ownership, in Chapter 3.

As a fox, her life is threatened. Folktales do not exist in isola-
tion. The story of the Jewel Maiden and other folktales about wild
foxes darken the view of the Japanese fox. Killing foxes has deep
roots in history: the Ainu word for fox translates to "what we
kill a lot."[30] Despite the dangers, she promises to visit the family
whenever her husband calls her name. The Japanese fox forms
permanent, monogamous relationships regardless of her love being another fox or a human.[31]

In every fox-wife story, she must leave the family or die. These
tales do not have happy endings. Most of the stories end with the
husband and children crying and begging her not to go. She turns
her tail and runs away, leaving only tears and memories behind.
But why must she leave or die? Why can't these tales have a happy
ending? She doesn't belong to the human world. While she tries
hard to become human for the sake of her lover and children, she
fails. She fails because she cannot fully participate in cultural and
economic life.[32]

In our story, the fox fears the puppy. Foxes and dogs have a
long-standing rivalry in folklore. This comes from a real rivalry.
Dogs hunt foxes. Beyond this, the puppy represents the natural
household order. The puppy reveals the fox's true form as she
goes about her duty of running the household: making sure la-

borers are well and working. In other fox-wife stories, her disguise disappears when handling the household finances and similar duties.

The lack of a happy ending in these folktales provides a balance. Fox-wives stories radiate with happiness and love but remain incomplete without sorrow. She must disappear to complete the fleeting beauty of the image. Doesn't this reflect what we too must experience in life? Even the most loving of relationships must end in separation: death. Punctuating romance with sorrow inspires a feeling of gratitude. This sense of gratitude and awe amid mystery pervades Japanese thinking. For example, Shinto rites are designed to invoke feelings of appreciation and emotion.[33]

Tales of fox-wives shine against the backdrop of negative proverbs and other negative stories centering on women. The fox-wife shows her flaws and lacks the ability to meet her social obligations, yet throughout Japan's history men desired her. She tries to be a divine mother and dutiful wife, yet she doesn't fit into society. She speaks about the condition of women in feudal Japan. Beyond this, she represents the soul of Japan and an expression of the Japanese world view.[34] Her story speaks of the human condition – inadequacy, ceaseless effort to improve, and separation. She lives on the boundary between two worlds, wholly belonging to neither. She cannot attain perfection and yet strives to improve. Just as each of us must leave our families, the fox-wife tale always ends in separation.

Shape-shifting and Head Shaving

The fox-wife is not the only type of shape-shifting story. The Japanese fox doesn't limit herself to the shape of a beautiful woman, nor are all Japanese foxes benevolent mothers-to-be. Fox folklore brims with sexy prankster fox-women and shifty trouble-makers. In the fox-wife stories, she uses her cunning to help her appear as human as possible. Many fox tales use the same characteristic to cause trouble for hapless humans.

But how exactly does the fox transform? The method varies. In some stories, the fox places a human skull on its head and bows to the stars until the skull doesn't fall off.[35] Another method of shape-shifting requires the fox to make a coat of leaves—no small feat for an animal without hands—and make a topknot out of a wisp of straw. Then she does three double somersaults without touching the ground.[36] Despite all the effort, the fox may not transform completely. Young foxes can't include their tails and lose their disguise whenever they get drunk or lose their concentration. Only old, wise foxes transform into beautiful fox-wives. Most prank tales feature a young fox.

What types of pranks does the fox enjoy? Well, wild foxes enjoy shaving the heads of unwary men. One such story, "The Carpenter and Foxes," shows just how tricky the Japanese fox can be.

One day a young carpenter named Toku travels to a moor named Maki. People know foxes infest the place, but Toku is a stubborn man and doesn't believe in the stories. His fellow carpenters dare him to enter the moor. If nothing happens, he will win a big bottle of *sake*, but if he loses he must buy each of his friends a bottle. Determined to show his friends how silly they are, he enters Maki. Soon after entering, he sees a fox transform itself into a beautiful girl by placing duckweed on its head. Toku decides to turn the tables on the foolish fox. When fox-girl calls out to him, asking for help returning to her village, Toku decides to play along. During the walk, he tries to see the end of the fox's tail peeking out from the fox girl's robes, but he doesn't have any luck.

They come upon the village and the fox's supposed house. Toku tells the resident couple about the fox-girl, but they fail to believe him. To prove he is right, he grabs the girl and demands she reveal her true nature. She stammers her confusion until Toku grabs a piece of wood and beats the girl to force her to reveal her tail. Only the girl never transforms. She collapses on the floor of her parent's house, broken and lifeless.

Horrified at what they have just witnessed, the parents drive Toku from their home. A Buddhist priest happens to be passing by and, hearing the wailing of the old couple, demands an explanation. The parents tell the priest about the murder and demand the young carpenter pay with his life. Toku collapses before the priest and pleads for mercy.

The Buddhist priest asks the parents to spare Toku's life so he may spend it trying to make amends as a discipline of Buddha. They relent. A grateful Toku kneels before the priest. The priest bids the mother to bring a razor and water to shave Toku's head, as is the custom to become a disciple. As soon as the last swipe of the razor lifts, Toku hears laughter, and he awakens to find himself sitting in the moor alone. He raises his hand to find his head has been shaved. He lost his bet.

Foxes often use people's knowledge against them. In the story, Toku knows about how foxes are shape-shifters despite not believing the stories. The fox lets Toku see her transform, knowing he will think he has the advantage. Then she uses his knowledge against him. Fox tales sometimes let the reader in on the fun, like this one. Anyone who is familiar with other fox tales will know Toku is in for it.

As you can see in the story, foxes cast illusions to complete the prank. The village, the parents, and the priest are all illusions cast by other foxes joining the fun. Illusion and shape-shifting play roles in a related tales about feasts.

One evening a traveler came across a beautiful woman. "You look exhausted from your journey," she said. "Please come to my house and rest."

The man was indeed tired from his long journey, and the woman was exceedingly beautiful, so he accepted. The woman's home was as exquisite as her figure. In the dining hall spread a feast like he had never beheld. Food of all types, some he had only heard about, piled the finest porcelain.

"Please, eat your fill," the beautiful hostess said. "I am quite alone and would enjoy your company for the night." The look on her face left no doubt to her intent.

The next morning, the traveler awoke to a cold, open sky. He sat upright and realized he lay in a muddy grave. Strewn around him were bones, leaves, and worse. He wiped his mouth, feeling sick. Laughter lilted on the wind.

In these stories, the fox leads the victim to a palace by a beautiful girl. A lavish feast spreads before him. After enjoying the feast, and sometimes the charms of the fox-girl, the man awakens in a grave surrounded by the feast's leftovers. Only instead of food, the poor guy sees rotting leaves, garbage, and feces.

The Price of Failure

Pranks do not always go well for the fox. Because young foxes cannot transform their tails, they are often discovered and killed. One such story tells of a silly fox who finds a *noh* mask. *Noh* masks represent characters in plays. Because of this, the fox thinks the mask will transform her. She slips it on her head and runs off to try to trick someone. Her first potential victim happens to be a hunter whose puzzlement only lasts a moment. The fox dies before she realizes her mistake.

Failed pranks have dire consequences. Discovered foxes die or even face exile. Another folktale accounts of one such exile.

"A fox took the shape of the consort of the Lord of Shikoku, and the latter found to his unbounded astonishment two women sitting in his house, who were exactly alike and who both pretended to be his real wife. A physician believed that it was the so-called 'soul-separating' illness, which causes one woman to become two. He uttered a Buddhist stanza and striking on the floor with his staff proceeded to recite prayers, but all in vain. Then the husband seized the women and shut them up. As he saw that one of them ate quite different food from the ordinary, he examined that one by torture, whereupon she became a fox. He then decided to kill the animal, but a crowd of 4 or 5000 people, Buddhist priests and laymen, men and women, came before the gate and answered the Lord's question, as to why they were, as follows:

"We are the foxes of the whole of Shikoku, who come to you with a request. The fox who has done you a wrong is a descendant of Kiko myojin, the 'Venerable Fox-god'; his name is Osa- gitsune, he is a messenger of Inari and the King of the Foxes of Japan. If you do him harm, there will come great calamity upon the country. He is our teacher of haunting, and if he dies we cannot haunt any longer. Please spare his life!' The Lord promised that if they all would leave Shikoku by ship, he would send the prisoner after them. Thereupon, they gave him a <u>written</u> oath, that they never would return to Shikoku as long as this document existed. They went away and since that time there have been no foxes in Shikoku. The document was, in the author's time, still in the hands of the same family."[37]

The story explains why Shikoku is one of the few islands in Japan that lacks foxes. Notice how not even the King of Foxes fits into human society. This motif appears in most stories where the fox poses as a human.

Wild fox tales are not limited to feudal Japan. In 1889, a train was seen on the Tokyo-Yokohama line, speeding toward other trains. The strange train would always remain the same distance and threaten a head-on collision. One night, a train engineer grew tired of this. He ramped up the speed of his train and caught up with the phantom. As soon as he closed the distance, the phantom train disappeared. A short time later, a crushed fox was found under the real train's wheels.[38]

Zen, the Senses, and the Fox

Fox disguises and illusions warn us about trusting our senses. The tales emphasize how easily our senses are tricked. Foxes can transform feces and garbage into a delicious feast. They can become trees, horses, and trains. Foxes transform to match desires. The beautiful girl people stumble across isn't what she appears. Desire and fox magic complete the illusion. The victim sees and hears what he wants. Fox illusions only work because the victim wants what the fox seems to offer. A story of a young samurai takes this idea to an extreme. In the story, the fox doesn't offer what the samurai desires, but he wants what he wants regardless.

A young samurai travels near Kyoto where he comes across a lovely girl dressed in silk. Struck by her beauty, he invites her into conversation. They talk deep into the night until the samurai confesses his love for her. He demands she returns his affection. She refuses and protests he is married. He continues to press her until she breaks down and cries. She tells him that having sex with him would lead to her death. He shrugs this off. After all, who ever heard of someone dying after having a tryst? She eventually gives in. When morning comes, she gets ready to go home. She tells him she goes home to die, and she asks him to visit her. She also asks him to copy the Lotus Sutra and offer it to Buddha for her soul's sake. He thinks the request is silly, but he promises anyway to put her at ease. Later, he travels to the girl's home with the hopes of seeing her again. Only he comes across her distraught mother. He goes up a hill and finds the body of a beautiful female fox. Upon seeing her, he knows the fox is the girl. Grief overwhelms the samurai, and he decides to keep his promise. He dutifully copies the sutra many times, feeling as if he couldn't do anything to right the wrong he committed. One night, the girl appears in a dream and thanks him for his hard work. His action saves her soul from the sin of the dalliance. The young samurai gains spiritual insight from the encounter and his work copying and memorizing the spiritual teachings of the sutra.[39]

The story contains strong Zen elements. The experience of the samurai helps him grow spiritually. The Lotus Sutra he copies contains the foundational teachings of Buddhism. Copying these teachings helps the samurai learn about how to act selflessly toward people. It is a fitting lesson for his selfish behavior toward the fox. Zen Buddhism embraced fox stories as teaching tools and enjoyed using those stories to break people out of their normal ways of thinking. These stories love to play with people's assumptions, and Zen uses the wild fox to represent people's lack of understanding.[40] Despite its usefulness in spiritual practice, belief in fox shape-shifting stories can lead people to disbelieve their senses in dangerous ways.

In 1889, Japan's Bandai volcano erupted, destroying a 27 square-mile area around it. A plume of debris and smoke rose 20,000 feet into the air. Lafcadio Hearn interviewed an old man who witnessed the event from a nearby peak. The old man thought the eruption, earthquakes, and black rain were all the work of a fox trying to trick him with an illusion.[41] In this case, the man deluded himself to avoid being tricked by a fox. The man couldn't believe what he saw and categorized it as a fox-illusion. The destruction didn't concern him because it wasn't real in his mind. This is similar to Toku in the story, "The Carpenter and Foxes." Both the old man and Toku relied on their knowledge of fox behavior, and both were mistaken. Hearn's account reveals how deep fox tales extend into Japanese culture. The stories provide a way to explain the unimaginable. The man was fortunate not to have stood closer to the "illusion."

Misunderstanding the Fox

Although the fox is deeply woven into Japan's culture, she remains misunderstood. A particularly cruel story accounts of a fox who is tortured because people misunderstood her intent and behavior.

Once, long ago, a fox in the shape of a girl asked passing riders if she mightd ride behind them to get home. Most riders agreed, and when the riders stopped at their destinations, the girl leaped off the horse in her fox form. Well, word of these antics made their way to a garrison of soldiers. Determined to end the mischief before it escalated—after all, who knew what such a bold fox would do next!—the officer of the garrison tricked the fox into a horse ride and captured her. He took her to the garrison where his fellow soldiers tried to shoot her with arrows, just for fun. She managed to escape by using her superior agility to jump around the arrows and over the wall. The officer went out and tricked the foolish fox into another horse ride. He captured her again and tortured her until she reverted to her true form. Afterward, the soldiers burned her and let her go. Sometime later, the officer found the fox in her female form and asked her if she wanted a ride. She refused.[42]

The soldiers worry about the fox's intention, and the fox simply enjoys riding on the back of a horse. Because the soldiers do not understand the fox's harmless—albeit annoying—behavior, they torture her. For the fox's part, she doesn't harm anyone other than perhaps scaring them out of their wits. But her antics push at social class divisions. Samurai lending rides to women, particularly women of lower class, hurts the samurai's reputation. Like many other fox-woman stories, this tale warns against picking up women who are alone. Remember, women had few rights in feudal Japan and were regarded as a type of property. Picking up a woman could be mistaken for theft. The men intend to take advantage of the fox-girl, and that intent leaves them open to public shame: being seen with a woman on his warhorse. The fox's desire for fun causes her to be tortured and disfigured.

As you can see, the Japanese fox is a complicated creature. Her ability to shape-shift makes her an ideal wife and a dangerous prankster. Luckily, most prankster foxes are unable to fully transform and have to rely on illusions. This gave her victims some chance of seeing through the prank. Not all foxes are tricksters, however. Some use their shape-shifting skills to help people. Foxes in these tales are motivated by a deep sense of gratitude toward a person. Their actions overlap the wild fox trickster's antics and the selfless love of the fox-wives. In many of these shape-shifting stories, the fox fails at her prank, but the victim shows mercy. Mercy is rare indeed for failed tricksters. Because of these tales, gratitude becomes a key trait of the Japanese fox.

Chapter 2
The Grateful Fox

Not all foxes are tricksters or divine wives; many fall into the gray area between. Many foxes have kind hearts and want to help people. Other foxes are tricksters who have a change of heart after being shown mercy. In most failed prank stories, such as Nakadayu and the fox-tree, the fox pays for her failure with her life. Pranksters know that failure means death, so when the victim shows mercy to the prankster, the fox becomes overwhelmed with gratitude. Appreciation often forces the fox to become less selfish. The debt changes her life.

Some foxes enjoy helping people, as long as their help is appreciated. One old man discovers what happens when a helpful fox feels snubbed.

An old man in Owari Province labors to dig a well. A kind-hearted fox sees how hard the old, bent-backed man worked and decides to help. The fox transforms into a strong young man and finishes digging the well in no time, but instead of nicely thanking the fox, the old man complains. Angry and disappointed with the old man's lack of appreciation, the fox curses the water in the new well.[43]

The Japanese fox's sense of ethics requires people to express gratitude whenever she helps them. She wants appreciation for using her powers for a person's benefit. If the person grumbles like the old man, the fox quickly feels fed-up and seeks revenge.

The other class of gratitude tales deals with people forgiving the fox. These stories stress the importance of mercy and compassion. Whenever a person spares her, the fox expresses gratitude through gifts. In some of these stories, fox gifts can be a bit mixed. Sometimes she will award money as thanks for the help, but half the money transforms into leaves or garbage because of the fox's nature. Shape-shifting and illusion are like breathing for a fox. Helping someone with expectation for a certain reward ends with disappointment. The tales reveal how many people never feel satisfied with what they have.

Gratitude motivates the Japanese fox to perform selfless acts that cost her life or the lives of her children. In traditional Chinese and Japanese medicine, the fox's liver and other organs were believed to cure some illnesses.[44] The use of fox-organs to cure people plays a role in a few gratitude fox-tales. One touching story shows the selflessness of a fox family.

> Long, long ago, a man delivered a fox-cub from the hands of some boys, who had caught it and were going to kill it. The little fox joyfully scampered away. Shortly afterward, the man's

only son fell seriously ill; all kinds of medicines were tried, and in the end, the physician decided that only the liver of a live fox could cure the boy. The parents tried in vain to obtain such a liver from the villagers—nobody had any. But late that night a stranger came to the house, bringing a fresh fox-liver which he said he had received for the boy. After eating it, the boy of course recovered, but the parents still did not know who might have sent them the liver until one night in a dream, the mysterious stranger again appeared to the father and explained that in gratitude for the earlier delivery of their cub, he and the mother had decided to kill it so that its liver might save the kind-hearted man's son. The parents, in turn, showed their gratitude by erecting a shrine to the Fox-*Inari* in their garden, where they prayed for the cub's soul, and venerated the fox couple.[45]

Gratitude moves the fox family to do whatever they can to repay the father's kindness. The Japanese fox suggests how we should feel toward the kindness people show us. Unlike the well-digging old man, the human father of this story expresses his gratitude by erecting a shrine to honor the sacrifice of the foxes. They realize the fox couple could never be repaid. By building a family shrine, the human father ensures that the fox couple's sacrifice would be remembered for as long as the father's lineage continues. In a similar story, an old man finds a pack of stray dogs eating a horse carcass. A starving, lame fox watches the grotesque feast. The old man feels sorry for the fox and drives the dogs away at great personal risk. The man cuts a slab of horse flesh and offers it to the fox, and the grateful fox teleports the old man to the fox's home. There, the fox's elderly parents give the man a book called the *Choni-soshi*. The book allows the man to understand the language of animals. Using the book, the old man learns about many things, such as how to help a wealthy woman struggling with a hard labor. The woman successfully gives birth and rewards the old man with so much money that he doesn't have to worry about material things again.[46]

As a creature that lives on the border of the human and animal world, the fox acts as a gatekeeper for animal knowledge. The lame, starving fox's family gives the kind old man the ability to access animal knowledge. They trust the man to use the knowledge to benefit others. Notice how the man doesn't set out to benefit from the fox's gift. Intention determines reward. As you may guess, if the man had fed the fox with the intention of getting something in return, the fox wouldn't have rewarded him. The Japanese fox rewards those who lack ulterior motives and punishes complainers and connivers. She repays kindness with kindness and loyalty, even when the person originally acts cruelly toward her. For example, people will sometimes take one of the fox's most precious possessions: her soul-pearl. Both Chinese and Japanese fox stories mention how fox souls live in a gem the fox carries with her. Chinese foxes carry their soul-pearl in their mouths; Japanese foxes carry theirs on the tip of their tails. As you can guess, people desire such a priceless gem. For a fox that has the gem stolen and returned, the word *gratitude* lacks the ability to express her feelings:

Once long ago lived a woman who was thought to be possessed by a fox. The woman would play with a mysterious, gem-like ball. She didn't cause any harm, but out of good caution, the villagers avoided her. One day a young samurai entered the village and witnessed the woman's play. In a flash, he snatched her ball out of the air and examined it. It was nothing like anything he had seen. The woman begged him to return the ball, saying she would protect him if he did. After the woman pleaded, cried, and threatened, the samurai relented and returned the strange plaything. The woman told him to call her by her name should he ever need her protection. Her name was *Kitsune*.

On his way home, the samurai suddenly felt dread. This deep foreboding chilled him. He knew he was in danger. But from where? After remembering the fox's promise, he called out her name. She appeared from nowhere and listened to the samurai's feelings. She too felt the danger crackling the air, and she walked ahead of him to sense the way. After walking for a time, she directed him to enter the bamboo forest and led the samurai on a winding trail. Then he saw them: Enemy samurai waited in the darkness to ambush him, but the cunning fox-protector led him around them and to safety. The samurai felt gratitude toward the fox. Over the course of the samurai's life, he had to call upon the fox for help on several more occasions. Each time she came and acted as his guardian angel.[47]

At first, the samurai acts cruelly. He steals the fox's soul and only relents after she threatens and cries. However, the fox feels grateful when the samurai returns her precious ball. She realizes he could have stolen the soul ball despite her threats. She repays his kindness in a way that transforms the young samurai. He realizes "that *Kitsune* was an animal very grateful, repaying the kindness of man." The revelation changs how the samurai treats people. Because foxes can shape-shift and cast illusions, everyone must be treated with kindness. After all, a stranger may well be a fox in disguise. People who act differently should also be treated with kindness. Again, they could be a fox. The likelihood of the person being a fox increases with the person's abnormal behavior. Western society inherited a similar idea from Christianity. People are called to be kind to others because the other person could be an angel in disguise.[48]

Modern Gratitude

Fox gratitude stories continue into the modern period and have some interesting twists. Like folktales, modern newspaper accounts of fox kindness are understood as a matter-of-fact. *Japan Chronicle* relates how a kindhearted fox helped a murder investigation in April 1923.

> Last August in a house near the Hanshin Terminus, right opposite to a police box, a whole family was done to death with an iron bar. The murder was discovered by a neighbor, and after all details had been widely published, the police forbade mention of it. Incidentally, the Chronicle was fined ¥30 for mentioning that a crime had been committed such was the strictness of the embargo, and there were, in consequence of this procedure, all sorts of rumors about a policeman being the culprit, these rumors being indignantly denied. Suspects were duly arrested and examined in the usual manner.
>
> Sometime after, at Onoye-dori, a fox was seen and chased and caught in a thicket, where an iron bar, believed to be the weapon with which the murders were committed, was discovered by the hunters. The fox was taken alive, and the Japanese papers reported that when he was produced in

the police station—of all extraordinary things to do—a man who was at that time under examination, trembled all over and made a clean breast of the crime.

The fox is still a captive but has been deified, and a shrine has been erected for him at Kurakuen, the pleasure resort on the Rokko hill-side. A few days ago the formal dedication ceremony was conducted in the presence of numerous local officials, policemen, and some Japanese newspaper representatives. The shrine has been provided in honor of the creature's 'having at the risk of his life suggested the whereabouts of the concealed weapon.' Anyhow the animal is attracting a number of devotees since his consecration at Kurakuen, including, it is said, police officials and detectives. The new shrine is adorned with the red *torii*, *sembon-nobori*, and other adornments peculiar to the shrine of Inari-san. Nothing, by the way, has been heard further of the man who confessed. Perhaps it did not turn out to be him after all, or perhaps he is in prison still awaiting trial. With a deified fox put in as evidence against him, he will have to prove a very good alibi to get off.[49]

This newspaper article reveals how people expressed gratitude toward the fox for her help: they built shrines. The act of building a shrine publicly honors the actions of the fox. The self-sacrificing fox-couple enjoyed the honor of having a shrine dedicated to them, and the guardian-angel fox and book-giving fox family express the same level of gratitude. The appreciation of the fox ties back to her unique place as the ideal wife. The fox-wife takes care of her family out of duty, love, and appreciation. The Japanese fox risked death with every human interaction. Welcoming a fox into the family as a wife creates the deepest feelings of gratitude. That sense of gratitude drives the fox to protect the samurai who stole the soul-pearl. It motivates the lame fox to give an old man the key to animal language.

However, fox gratitude has a hidden dark side. The common thread shared by the positive gratitude stories involves fox shrines or fox guardianship. The family becomes associated with the fox, and this association becomes trouble. In later periods of Japanese history, families with a history of fox dealings face a label: fox-owners. What was once a benefit becomes a serious problem, a problem that still plagues some families in Japan.

Chapter 3
Fox in the Family

Fox-ownership doesn't involve actually owning a fox. Fox-adoption would be a better phrase. Anyway, do you remember the story of the fox-cub from the previous chapter? The fox family chooses to help the human family. The family doesn't strike a deal with the fox family; the fox family simply acts. Fox-ownership builds on this autonomy. Stories of wild fox trickery create the foundation for fox-ownership. One of the most famous of these stories links the fox with ill-gotten wealth: "The Lucky Teakettle." There is another story of the same name that features the other shape-shifter in Japanese folklore, the *tanuki*.

The story tells of a man who saves a fox from death. To repay the kindness, the fox uses its shape-shifting powers to transform into various objects for the man to sell for a nice sum. After each sale, the fox eventually returns, assumes a new shape, and is sold again. Money pours into the man's pocket. Eventually, the man becomes a village elite. The poor fox, on the other hand, pays for the man's increasing social status. When the fox transforms into a teakettle, the priest who bought the teakettle tries to put it to use. Burned, the fox reverts to her true form and runs, yelping away. Later, a feudal lord buys the fox disguised as a horse. Despite appearances, the fox is still just a fox and unable to bear a human rider. The disappointed and disgusted lord dumps the exhausted fox-horse into a muddy ditch.[50]

In the story, the fox sacrifices herself for the man's benefit because of his altruism. She does this without the man's prompting. The story shows how foxes have a sense of honor, but that honor isn't as well developed as a person's sense of honor. She doesn't hesitate to trick others out of money. This behavior sets the stage for fox-ownership stories.

Money and Fox-ownership

During the 17th and 18th century, many farmers and merchants followed a teakettle path to the aristocracy. During this time, Japan moved away from rice as currency and toward coins.[51] As society shifted to money as a currency, some farmers and merchants were able to capitalize on the change. This had moral implications. Feudal Japanese considered wealth as a reward for good acts. That also meant an evil action plunged you into poverty.[52] However, the rapid rise of neighbors mixed jealousy with admiration. Fears about changing village dynamics led to people labeling these wealthy neighbors as fox-owners.

New, rapid wealth revived stories like the "Lucky Teakettle". Many people began to realize families who had dealings with foxes in their past were among those who gained wealth. Jealousy, fear, folklore, and family history combined into the fox-ownership label.

Money and the Threat to Tradition

About the width of a fox's paw separated the new currency and past concepts of wealth. At the time, currency undermined folk beliefs. Farmers believed any object or tool could gain a spirit through age and use. For example, feudal farmers held memorial services for long-used needles. The needles became alive through their long use by a single family. You may be more familiar with the idea of a sword gaining a spirit than sewing needles, as samurai movies make a fuss of their sword spirits. It's the same idea. Farmers didn't believe needles could speak, feel, or think. The needles were still needles, but they did gain a sort of spiritual power that demanded respect. Memorial services put the spirit in the needle to rest and expressed appreciation for the needle's service. Hammers, knives, and other kitchen utensils needed similar send-offs. A priest would chant a sacred text as the needles were cremated or set adrift on a river.[53] In contrast, money didn't have an owner or the ability to gain a spirit. A coin couldn't have a single owner like a needle. Money was a lifeless thing, and folk beliefs struggled with this gap before settling on the fox as the spirit that should be connected to money. Currency couldn't fit into the rural way of thinking without this association. Already, the fox had many stories dealing with wealth. She was also associated with Inari, the goddess of rice. These ideas mixed with fears of social upheaval and created the negative label of fox-ownership.

The Price of Being Adopted by a Fox

Fox owning families were shunned and excluded from community life because of the nature of their foxes. The fact that foxes stole the family's wealth didn't concern villagers as much as the threat of spiritual possession and trickery. People believed foxes acted on the owner's anger, jealousy, or resentment without any orders from the owner. People avoided fox-owners to keep from accidentally upsetting them and unknowingly bringing down the fox's wrath. Fox-owners were kept out of community life because of how fox-ownership was contracted.

There are five ways for a family to become fox-owners. First, as we have already seen, a fox may adopt a family out of gratitude for saving its life or some other good deed. The second method is through birth. Being born into a fox-owning family labels a person as a fox-owner for life. Escape can only be found by shoving a blade into the stomach—or jugular if you happen to be a woman. Moving is an option. After all, not everyone in Japan knows every winner of the fox lottery. The third way is through marriage. Marrying a fox-owner marries the fox. Marriage gives you in-laws and in-foxes. Trouble is, divorce doesn't free you from the fox. Once a fox-owner, always a fox-owner.[54]

The fourth method involves land. Buying land from fox-owners blesses the buyer with the fox's beneficial curse. Let me illustrate. Let's say a young man named Takeshi moves into a village several miles from Edo (modern-day Tokyo).

Takeshi wants to spend money on a weekend home. He finds a quaint house for sale by the owners and buys it outright. Soon after moving in, he notices neighbors and townspeople avoid him. He tries to get involved with the community, but he gets witheringly polite looks. He discovers that the family who owned the home had a fox. Luckily, several rice paddies away another home hits the market, this one owned by the local bank. Takeshi foists the fox-home on a colleague and buys the bank-owned home. Soon after, the village warms to him.

What happened?

The transfer of the fox's wealth—land in this case—labels Takeshi as a temporary fox-owner. As long as he owns the land, the community wants nothing to do with him. Temporary fox-owners even risk being thrown out of their families to avoid spreading the fox-ownership disease. Luckily, Takeshi doesn't have to worry about this because he doesn't have family in the village. Buying a fox-home muddies the reputation of the entire family. This taboo on buying land of families that became rich in the 17-18th centuries protects the wealth of those families.

Years pass. Takeshi begins to use his wealth to work his way into the village council. A man from Edo could offer much to a village. Besides, Takeshi wants the village to prosper. A proper stone wall would attract merchants and keep some of the Shogun's darn dogs out. Suddenly, his relationships with his neighbors ice. Close friends keep having something come up whenever

Takeshi plans a card night. Oh, everyone still acts politely. Perhaps a touch too polite. He remembers his first time in the village. The realization chills him. No one would tell him to his face, of course. Japanese society is too civil for that. Just the same, Takeshi knows what people say about him: fox-owner. But how? His land doesn't have a fox!

Our Takeshi stumbles across the last way of becoming a fox-owner. Feudal Japanese villages frowned upon using wealth to buy social influence. A young upstart like Takeshi posed a danger to a village's established hierarchy. In order to prevent new wealth from corrupting politics, people who overstepped themselves with their money were labeled fox-owners.[55] Councils kept villages in order by creating rules about how taxes for the local lord were collected and regulating their own militia.[56] New wealth like Takeshi, regardless if they came from outside or inside the village, threatened a village's self-governance. Slapping the fox-owner label on such—sometimes well-meaning—wastrels segregated them from the rest of the village. The label placed them under special sets of rules that kept the fox-infection from spreading.

Despite newly rich families gaining the label of fox-owners centuries ago, the idea of owning a fox still influences marriage in modern Japan. Our fictional Takeshi's descendants would suffer from his mistake. In 1952, a young man's family forbade his marriage because his fiancé came from a fox-owning family. The young couple decided to die together instead of facing a life apart or a marriage of shame.[57] Fox-ownership isn't as rare as you may think. The town of Kamo in Shimane Prefecture has 10% of its families labeled as fox-owners.[58]

Why Call People Fox-owners?

For those of us in the West, the label seems silly. But the separation of these families from the rest of the community attempts to retain social harmony. It prevents these wealthy families from taking control of the village. But being a fox-owner isn't all muck and manure; the label protects rich families from the jealousy of less-fortunate neighbors. All the negative aspects of being a fox-owner help keep envy in check. Fox-ownership protects the family's wealth *and* the interests of the community.

Speaking of wealth, how can land be sold and bought without gaining the fox-owner label? After all, eventually some of these families will need to sell or rent their land. This, too, needs to be done in a way that keeps the social fabric of the village harmonious. Luckily, fox-ownership rules provide a loophole: government officials may buy land without a problem. They have the ability to drive foxes away, allowing the land to be bought and sold without worrying about the fox. I guess foxes dislike government? Actually, the rule protects the community's harmony. It keeps debt in the hands of a third party instead of in the hands of neighbors. Debt held within a community can fester into resentment and other problems. Imagine owing someone you see every day a large amount of money. Now imagine many people owing money to that neighbor. Pretty soon, he will become wealthier than his neighbors. This was the same path many new-money families strolled when currency was adopted. To prevent this, villages started allowing the government to sell land and keep the community's balance from toppling.

Fox-ownership protects the community from itself. The practice of separating fox-owners helps protect those families from having problems with their neighbors and protects the fox-owning family's land. Of course, it isn't all rice and cherry blossoms for those rich families. Fox-ownership forces the wealthy to look at other villages for marriage partners or risk a lover's suicide. Fox-ownership, like all aspects related to the Japanese fox, balances between positive and negative.

Villagers feared fox-owners because of the threat of fox-possession. A possession in the Shogun's family drove the mighty Hideyoshi to write a letter to the priests of Inari. If it drove the most powerful man in Japan to seek help, you can understand why a peasant would fear possession. Fox possession gave the fox-owner label teeth.

Chapter 4
Fox Within: Fox Possession

Suddenly, you crave it. The thought of its stringy, lean flesh—battered and fried until a crispy brown—makes you drool. Yes, those shriveled ears taste divine. The crunch of bones. Sublime. Rice and red beans. The rice sops up the oils from the main course. And red beans. They go so very well with a fried rat.

You, my friend, have just been possessed by a wild fox.

Fox possession appears in Japan during the 11th century.[59] Chinese fox stories speak about possession, but the Japanese stories develop this ability far beyond their original Chinese inspiration. *Kitsune-tsuki* (pronounced *key-tzoon-nay tzoo-key*) is the second most famous ability of the Japanese fox—shape-shifting being the best known. The two types of foxes (divine and wild) war with each other over who controls the minds of humans. Wild foxes delight in possessing people. Divine foxes, Inari foxes in particular, are charged with keeping their sisters in line. Poker chips change from paw to paw. Human well-being and society anted-up. The wild fox smirks, and her divine elder sister wags her nine tails in warning. In feudal Japan, I envision them playing *go*.

Nowadays, poker would likely be their game of choice. Inari fox and wild sister played a game as recently as 1978.

Takao lived through a car accident when he was eighteen years old. Soon after the accident, he started imitating a fox. He would jump around and shout. He was found walking the streets dressed in a raincoat and a helmet, carrying a huge sickle. After several unhelpful hospital visits, his family believed he was possessed and tied him up in a storehouse to keep him from hurting himself. Various priests tried to exorcise him but failed; back to the hospital's padded room he went. He was deemed to be in an acute psychotic state and treated with a tranquilizer. After a month of medical treatment and seeing religious practitioners, he recovered.[60]

On the surface, fox possession appears to be a form of hysteria or mania. In the early 1900s, it was classified as such. However, many researchers think defining fox possession using Western terms removes it from its cultural and social context. In other words, becoming fox-possessed requires living in villages with fox beliefs. It differs from being simply manic or schizophrenic.[61]

The Disease of Fox Possession

Fox possession was considered a disease by Japan's feudal doctors. They defined two types of wild foxes: low-class and high-class. Low-class foxes were less sophisticated and understood human culture poorly. Because of this lack of understanding, possession by these foxes resulted in bizarre behavior. Victims of these foxes broke social norms and often acted like foxes like Takao did. They ate food associated with foxes such as red beans and rice and fried tofu.[62] Most cases of possession were associated with this type of fox. The word *possession* refers to "when normal, everyday thinking is overturned."[63]

High-class fox possession was harder to spot. This type of possession could even benefit the victim. High-class wild foxes were older and understood human culture better than their low-class sisters. The fox mimicked the victim's behavior so well that differences were barely noticeable.[64] The person also gained the ability to write in languages he didn't know. Often, the only giveaway to the possession were these sudden hidden skills and knowledge.

In both types of possession, the victim could speak with the fox spirit. High-class foxes formed a type of symbiotic relationship. That isn't to say low-class foxes weren't influenced by their host. Low-class foxes could develop into high-class foxes if the host trained spiritually. During Matsuoka Etsuko's study of a shaman and a cult in 1983, a case of a low-class fox possession transformed into a divine fox symbiosis.

Michiko was a 43 year old woman who complained about foxes making noise. A shaman held a ritual to help Michiko. Michiko dreamed of her ancestors who were dissatisfied. Foxes numbered among them. The shaman and Michiko held a memorial ritual over the course of seven days. The ritual seemed to work. However, three months later Michiko changed, and tension with the shaman developed. She eventually stopped visiting the shaman but continued her spiritual practices and seeking help from Etsuko and other psychologists. Over this time, she reported speaking with the fox. The fox helped her remember a fire that left her scarred when she was a child. In 1986, Michiko claimed the wild fox spirit had become a divine creature. The possession became a positive, symbiotic relationship in her view. The psychologists viewed it as schizophrenia. However, Michiko became a shaman herself after several years of spiritual practice. The practice transformed the wild fox into a divine fox that allowed Michiko access to its spiritual powers.[65]

What appeared to be schizophrenia ended in Michiko's attainment of a high religious status in her religious sect. Foxes were thought to change into divine beings whenever their hosts underwent spiritual practices. Michiko's treatment followed a standard practice, as most fox exorcisms involved various spiritual rituals and practices. Fox spirits were thought to be displeased because of something the host's ancestors did. Most of the time—as in Michiko's case—an ancestor murdered the fox. Memorial ceremonies were held to honor the fox and put it to rest. Michiko's spiritual training aimed at disciplining and educating the fox instead of exorcising it.

Michiko's fox developed into a divine being through her training, but without training, the fox could have become harmful.[66]

Many victims of fox possession seek both Western medical treatment and spiritual treatments. Traditional treatments lost their power over the fox, but Western psychology lack the spiritual dimension many people need. Neither traditional treatment nor can Western medicine treat fox possession on its own.[67]

Traditional treatment didn't always involve benign spiritual practices like meditating under a waterfall. In 1926, two women were killed by their family in an attempt to drive out the women's foxes. The family members filled the mother's and daughter's eyes and noses with sulfur.[68] Other traditional exorcism practices involve beatings and the use of torture. These practices come from folklore. Practices used to force a fox to resume her true shape also served to drive her spirit out of people. Some of these so-called treatments can be understood as punishment for how outspoken fox possession victims are.

The Benefit of Possession

Feudal Japanese society was highly stratified. People were expected to perform certain roles based on their genders and social statuses. Foxes ignored social status and inhabited people from all levels of Japanese society. However, farmers and women were afflicted most often.[69] Wrestlers had little to worry about. Foxes feared wrestlers as much as they feared dogs. Unlike wrestlers and dogs—one Shogun decreed killing a dog was murder—both farmers and women lacked a voice in feudal Japanese society. Possession allowed women to speak out without penalty, unless you count some traditional exorcist practices as punishment. Generally, people believed the fox spoke through its victim. Because foxes do not understand human social norms, a possessed person could become agitated over things that other people didn't consider important. The possessed person would also speak publically of private matters, much to the embarrassment of everyone. These characteristics gave unprecedented freedom to those who normally lived under tight social rules. Wives were prone to possessions. The fox allowed them to take a break from the difficult duties of being wives and speak out against their husbands' families with less risk of punishment.[70] The victim lashed out against injustices. Combining this threat with other fox traits gave women social power normally reserved for men. This transfer of social power can be found in Chinese stories. In these stories, the fox seduces the wife, but this seduction benefits the family and gives the wife power over the family. I will paraphrase one such story:

In the Jiajing period, a fox seduces the wife of a Dezhou man named Zhou. When he discovers this, it troubles him until his wife starts telling the fox what they lack. Soon, these items appear at the house, and Zhou's family grows wealthy. And the fox, speaking through the wife, offers business advice that benefits the family. To honor his wife's fox lover, Zhou builds a den for the fox behind the family home. Years later, his grandson forgets why this pile of straw sits behind the house and plans to build his room over the spot. In response, the fox (through the grandson's possessed wife) threatens to make the family poor. The terrified grandson replaces the den and makes it larger. Satisfied, the fox continues seducing new wives and bringing riches.[71]

Imported stories like this influenced both the idea of fox-ownership and the public view of possession. Possession was seen as negative. Wild fox possession led to erratic behavior. However, through spiritual training, a wild fox taking up residence in a wife could become a source of wealth or spiritual power. A high-class fox benefited a family. Because of these possibilities, fox possession was viewed as a mixed curse and blessing. Revealing a family's private matters caused problems, but for many, the wealth such possession brought may have been worth it. Fox possession provided a way for the wife to become an important figure in the household, just like Zhou's wife. Using possession as a means to speak out against society and family wasn't unique to Japan. Hysteria had long been known in the West as a tool that allowed people to criticize social norms and express discontent without punishment.[72]

Culture-Bound Hysteria

Modern psychology likes to categorize fox possession as hysteria, but this label poses problems. Fox possession is a culture-bound syndrome. Shoving the disease into a Western category denies the heritage fox possession has in Japanese and Chinese folklore. The label breaks the link between possession, family history, and the experiences the victims express while afflicted with a fox.[73] That said, the Western idea of hysteria provides some insight on how fox possession involves more than just the individual and her family.

While China shares stories of fox spirits inhabiting people, Japanese stories go far beyond their inspiration. These stories provide the groundwork for mass hysteria. Everyone in a village knows the stories and knows what possession can look like. It's similar to witch stories found in Medieval Europe. People blamed witches for outbreaks of hysteria in the same way rural Japanese villagers blamed foxes. All cultures report cases of mass hysteria, and it affects women more often than men. No one knows why.[74]

Dr. Shinshi Kadawaki in the 1890s found three conditions necessary for fox possession. First, the person had to know fox stories and believe those stories. Next, the person needed to grow up in an area where belief in fox spirits and stories were common. Finally, the person needed to lack skepticism.[75] The beliefs that led to outbreaks of hysteria also provided solutions. Traditional treatments of fox possession often involved public acts, such as Michiko's memorial service and spiritual training. These public treatments included the entire village, and the treatment drew on the common understanding of what a fox is. All of this contributes to an outbreak of hysteria.

Stories of fox possession share many similarities to what happened in Salem Massachusetts during the witch trials. Two young girls, Betty Parris and her cousin Abigail Williams, screamed, threw things, contorted, and other signs of possession. The entire town listened to Betty and Abigail's accusations and acted upon them. The town was caught up in hysteria. For young girls in a society where women held little authority, this must have been a heady experience. They could speak their minds without punishment. Japanese women possessed by foxes experienced similar freedom within their families.

The hysteria of fox possession threatened the fabric of a village and its families. When a member of Shogun Hideyoshi was possessed, mass hysteria became a national concern. The Shogun realized this and dispatched a letter to one of the most prominent Inari shrines:

> To the Inari God:
>
> Ukita's daughter is now babbling, apparently possessed by a wild fox. I hope that the fox will be dispersed immediately. When no suitable measures are taken, a nation-wide fox hunt will be ordered.
>
> P.S.
>
> The chief priest of the Yoshida Shrine was also notified concerning this matter.
>
> Hideyoshi[76]

The household of the Shogun wouldn't stoop to stuffing a daughter's eyes and nose with sulfur. Other deaths caused by well-meaning family members of fox victims forced the feudal Japanese government to push people toward trained priests and exorcists. If even the Shogun had to beseech the god Inari for help, what could a peasant family expect to do on their own?

The Shogun threatened Inari with a nation-wide fox hunt should the fox fail to leave his adopted granddaughter. This suggests how news of the fox could spread across the whole of Japan, and it shows how possession was a serious matter. A nation-wide fox hunt would consume a vast amount of resources and time. At the same time, such a hunt would dispel any mass hysteria outbreaks the news may cause. Luckily, the letter seemed to work. Hideyoshi didn't have to order the nation-wide fox hysteria-fueled hunt after all.

Hideyoshi's letter links wild foxes with the god Inari. What does the goddess of rice have to do with foxes and fox possession?

Chapter 5
Fox and Rice

The association of the fox with the god of wealth and rice is unique to Japan. Chinese divine foxes, the nine-tails, are associated with good omens, but unlike Japanese nine-tailed foxes, they are not the messengers of a popular god. Inari is the most popular deity in Japan. Conservative estimates number between 20,000 and 30,000 public Inari shrines. Many homes also have their own small shrines.[77] Who is Inari? And how did the Japanese fox become so closely associated with this god?

Inari's History

Inari began as a local deity of the Kyoto area. His first shrines appeared in the 8th century. Built on three hills overlooking the fertile Kamagawa plains, Inari was just one of several local harvest gods.[78] Over time, he absorbed the other deities in the area. Inari began as the god of rice, but because rice was used as a currency he also became closely associated with wealth. Rice served as the symbol of agriculture and of life in ancient Japan. Rice underpinned the whole of Japanese society. Any god associated with rice would become one of the most important deities simply because of the importance of rice.

Like the fox stories that eventually intertwined with Inari, rice came from China. Rice is a species of grass that can be grown anywhere with ample water. In feudal Japan, people ate rice for every meal, and the plant was used to make flour, alcohol, vinegar, and other products. Inari didn't become the most popular god until the Heian period (645-1185), and he remains the most popular deity in modern Japan.[79]

Time and the telling of his stories gradually changed Inari's gender from male to female. In official mythology, Inari is male but in the popular imagination, Inari is female.[80] Inari's first shrine has an interesting founding story. Because of the age of this story, Inari is referred to as male.

A proud, rich man liked to use *mochi,* rice cakes, as targets for his archery practice. One day, the soul of the Rice-god had enough. He transformed into the shape of a great white bird and flew away. The rich man saw the bird and became scared at the bad omen. He consulted an oracle about what he witnessed. The oracle told the rich man he would lose all of his wealth because of his wickedness and insults toward the Rice-god. In the hope to make amends and avoid his fate, the rich man built a shrine to the Rice-god on Mount Inari, where the rich man lived.[81]

In the earliest shrine stories, we can already see Inari's power over rice and wealth. Japanese deities are commonly named after the areas in which they live. Inari is named after Mount Inari.

It can be difficult to determine which name came first: the land or the god. Did you notice how foxes are not mentioned? Inari and the Japanese fox didn't become associated until later. Some of the earliest elements of Inari beliefs foreshadow the traits the Japanese fox developed. For example, neglecting sacred trees or a shrine dedicated to Inari leads to punishment, and the punishment most often involves madness that resembles fox possession.[82] Once the fox became associated with Inari, foxes began to appear in these stories.

Fox and Goddess

When I started my research, I thought it odd how the Goddess of Rice and the Japanese fox were related. After all, what does a fox have to do with rice and farming? Quite a bit, I learned. Foxes hunt in farmers' fields and pass between farmsteads and forests with ease. The fox's status as a boundary creature gives the fox special abilities beyond what we've already seen.[83] The fox tails are thought to be magic. As a fox runs through crops hunting rodents, frogs, and other food, their tails fertilize the field. This belief in fox-tail magic isn't isolated to Japan. European fox folktales share this belief. Despite these beliefs, farmers in Japan and Europe do not hesitate to set dogs on foxes that overstay their welcome. The conflict between dogs and foxes begins here. This belief in a magical fox tail provides a foundation for the fox's later association with Inari.

How the fox actually became associated with Inari is a mystery. However, one particular folktale explains how the Japanese vixen became a divine messenger.

> To the north of the capital, Kyoto, there lived a pair of very old white foxes in the neighborhood of Funaoka hill. The he-fox was a silver-white-furred animal and looked as if he were wearing a garment of bristling silver needles. He always kept his tail raised while walking. The she-fox had a deer's head with a fox's body. Their five cubs would follow them wherever they went. Each of these cubs had a different face.

> During the Koin Era, the two white foxes, accompanied by the five cubs, made their way to the Inari shrine at Fushimi, leaving their earth near Funaoka hill. When they reached Mount Inari on which the shrine stood, they prostrated themselves in front of the shrine and said reverently:

> "O Great God! We are naturally gifted with wisdom though we were born as animals. Now we sincerely wish to do our part of the peace and prosperity of the world. We regret, however, that we are not able to realize our purpose. O, Great God!

We pray from the bottom of our hearts that you would graciously allow us to become members of the household of this shrine so that we will be able to realize our humble wish!"

Greatly impressed by the sincerity with which these words were spoken, the sacred altar of the shrine instantly shook as if by an earthquake. And the next moment, the foxes heard the solemn voice of the Inari God coming from behind the sacred bamboo screen:

"We are always endeavoring to find some means to bestow the divine favor of Buddha on all men by doing our best. Your desire, foxes, is really praiseworthy. We will allow you, all of you, to stay here to do your service in this shrine forever. We expect you to assist with sympathy the worshipers and the people in general with the faith. We order you, He-Fox, to serve at the Upper Temple. We give you the name of Osusuki. And you, She-Fox, shall serve at the Lower Temple. We give you the name of Akomachi."

Hereupon each of the foxes including the five cubs made ten oaths and began to comply with the wishes of all the people.[84]

Did you notice how Inari spoke of Buddha? Shinto beliefs—Inari is a Shinto goddess—mix with Buddhist beliefs in ways that make them difficult to separate. I will avoid that rabbit hole, but it is important to mention. It suggests how fox folklore, Shinto beliefs, and Japanese Buddhism entangle. The foxes in the story are already divine white foxes. These foxes are also compassionate—they want to help people. The story tells us that Inari foxes are wise and desire to help. The Koin era dates between 810 and 823 AD, about the same time fox stories first appear in Japanese literature. The folktale suggests Inari and foxes became associated soon after the stories emigrated from China. The Japanese fox existed in oral telling long before the written collections circulated.

In any case, the story gives Inari a family of messengers. All religions have some sort of messenger that goes between God and humanity. For example, Christianity has Jesus, the Holy Spirit, and angels who act as messengers. As Inari grew from a local harvest god to the Goddess of Rice for all of Japan, she needed messengers. The folktale of the fox family appears just as Inari's popularity explodes. The most storied animal became associated with the most important crop in Japan.

Responsibilities of Divinity

Inari foxes are not mere wild foxes. They do not play tricks or possess people. However, they are charged with reining their wild sisters and punishing evil-doing humans. This is why Hideyoshi sent a letter to Inari when his adopted granddaughter was possessed. It's a pity people can't see the sisters in such encounters. Possession stories blandly speak of the Inari fox driving out the wild fox. Details about how this is done are rare. I picture the scenes as something like this:

The majestic, gleaming Inari fox stands over her ruddy, smirking sister. The Inari's nine tails slap her irritation. "Again, you play this trick?"

The red fox shrugs. "Humans are fun."

The Inari fox growls and lunges, forcing the red fox away from the hapless human. "Until one day I cannot save you. You can die, after all, even as a spirit."

The red fox laughs and bounds away. She pauses and looks at her divine sister. "I am too smart for their kind."

The Inari fox sighs.

Priests and families troubled by foxes call upon Inari. Inari's name acts as a talisman against wild foxes. At night, people will not refer to a fox by her name *Kitsune*. They fear the word will call an evil fox. People use word *Inari* instead. Let me clarify this. Not all wild foxes are evil. We've seen plenty of good foxes in our stories. The word *kitsune* is neutral. It can call an evil fox or a helpful fox. However, the word *Inari* will call only good foxes associated with the goddess.

Fox Statue or a Cat?

Beckoning fox statues surround public Inari shrines. These stone foxes carry scrolls in their mouths or sheaves of rice stalks. You can also see tiny versions of these beckoning statues in shops. Only these aren't foxes; they are cats. In fact, shops around major Inari shrines sell these little cats. These porcelain statues, known as beckoning cats, are favorite talismans of *geisha,* prostitutes, and shop owners. A white body with black splotches suggests fur. It sits on its haunches and raises its left paw. Around its neck wraps a silk ribbon with various ornaments. Like the fox, the cat statue invites wealth. However, cats are not usually associated with wealth, but a story from the 17th century links the cat, fox, and money together.

During the early Tokugawa period, a prostitute by the name of Usugamo loved cats. She owned so many that she required a maid to carry her pets wherever she went. People whispered of bewitchment. Usugamo's pimp demanded she rid herself of the cats. She refused. One day, a cat made a fuss while Usugamo visited her master. The cat meowed and tugged at her dress. The angry pimp drew a sword and beheaded the cat. The head flew up into the ceiling and caught a poisonous snake sliding down a support beam, saving both Usugamo and her master. The devastated

Usugamo held a funeral for the cat and invited the entire red-light district. Afterward, she fell into a deep depression and refused to leave her room. Not one of her other cats could comfort her. One of her wealthy regular customers felt terrible for her. The man ordered a carving of the cat in expensive wood with a waving left paw. So exquisite was the gift that Usugamo broke out of her deep depression. She became so happy that she attracted more patrons than she did before. Over time, she became famous and wealthy. Soon other prostitutes and shopkeepers began to copy Usugamo's cat statue in the hopes of having similar success. [85]

At first, I thought it odd that cats and foxes are symbols for fortune. After all, Inari foxes cannot be mistaken for cats. Inari fox statues look different from Japanese cat statues. However, while foxes can transform into cats, the relationship between feline and fox stretches further. In Chinese fox lore, foxes resemble cats.[86] In many regards, foxes resemble cats more than dogs. Foxes are solitary like cats rather than social hunters like wolves and dogs. Vertical pupils reflect light at night, and they stalk their prey similarly to a cat. Brightly-colored fox fur resembles the bright colorations of cats more than most dogs. Instead of hunting large prey like wolves, the fox seeks prey smaller than itself. Like cats, foxes are natural enemies of dogs.[87] Folktales emphasize these similarities. One Japanese folktale involving a fox trying to bewitch a rooster—foxes don't limit their pranks to humans—shows the fox assuming the pose of the beckoning cat:

One evening a man, Ito by name, living in Tajima Province heard a tumult coming from a flock of chickens left feeding in a mulberry field at the back of the house.

He went out of the house and looked around. A rooster was going tottering toward a bamboo grove in the neighborhood.

Then he saw a fox in the shade of a big tree near the bamboo grove. The fox was standing on its hind legs and beckoning to the rooster with one of its paws after the manner of the *maneki-neko* [beckoning cat statue].

The fox was apparently trying to bewitch the rooster through its hypnotic power. But when Ito shouted, the fox vanished into the bamboo grove. Then the rooster, he saw, went in the direction of the house with unsteady steps.[88]

With stories about the fox's relationship with riches, the fox's shape-shifting ability, the fox's cat-like traits, and stories like "Fox Bewitching a Rooster", I can understand why folklore confuses foxes with cats. The cat benefits the most from this confusion. Fox statues around Inari shrines draw from both the powers of aged, white foxes and their status as messengers of the goddess. Some of this power rubs off on these lucky cat statues because of how much foxes behave like cats. Buying a statue near an Inari shrine is a bonus. Many shops in Japan also have small shrines dedicated to Inari. These shrines contain a statue of a squatting fox with its right paw, rather than its left, beckoning.[89]

The Job of the Inari Fox

Several stories speak of Inari foxes rewarding people. In one story, a samurai asks for silver and gold in return for forbidding a retainer from killing foxes. The fox messenger tells the samurai that riches make a man unhappy. Instead, the fox gives the samurai a reward proper to his social status: land. Riches and wealth differ. Riches are short-term gains, such as gold and silver. Wealth lasts and continues to generate riches. The samurai's reward generated rice each year. This is a greater long-term reward than money.

Inari foxes relay prophecies and warnings from Inari in dreams.[90] But the ability of foxes to foresee danger and warn people extends beyond Inari foxes. Japanese fishermen listen to fox barks to determine the prospects for the coming day.[91] The tone and type of bark betray whether the fox is good or bad. Good foxes suggest a good day of fishing. Japanese and Ainu fisherman determine the weather based on these barks. While this appears to be another folk superstition, foxes really do bark to warn other foxes of inclement weather.[92]

Fishermen listened to barks, and other people asked Inari foxes for help with possession or other fox tricks. But there are people who wanted more. They wanted to command the many abilities of the fox. Such people are known as fox-sorcerers.

Chapter 6
The Sorcerer and the Fox

Some enterprising people discovered how to tap into the fox's powers whenever they wanted. They convinced the wild fox to become a spiritual familiar through her sense of gratitude. Are you ready to learn how to catch your very own fox-familiar? Best go fry some rats!

First, a wannabe fox-sorcerer needs to find a pregnant fox in her den. Next, ready that fried rat and muster your patience. You have to feed the pregnant fox and protect her over the course of her pregnancy. If you prove to be an excellent caretaker, she will offer one of her kits. You then need to name your new familiar. Calling your familiar's name summons her. Now the sorcerer needs to wait for his familiar to grow into an adult. Sounds good, right? There are some catches. Fox-familiars won't stand for a promiscuous, lewd, or greedy master. You can only keep one familiar and cannot use your familiar to assuage your greed. The fox may also leave if she finds your conduct offensive. [93]

There you have it! Just be careful not to get bitten while feeding the mother fox or deluded by one of her pranks!

Unlike fox-owners, fox-sorcerer families cannot pass a fox to descendants. Fox-owners and fox-sorcerers enjoy the powers of foxes, but there is an important difference; the fox chooses fox-owners regardless of the family's thoughts on the matter. Fox-sorcerers, on the other hand, seek and court foxes.

The earliest account of fox-sorcery appears in 1420. Shogun Ashikaga Yoshimichi discovered four members of his court were fox-sorcerers. The Shogun called exorcists to drive the familiars from the palace and exiled the perpetrators.[94]

Pipe Foxes

Shinano Province has a unique type of fox-familiar: the pipe fox. Unlike the fox-familiars of Ashikaga's reign, pipe foxes are a special, small breed of wild fox. They hide in the sleeve of their masters' robes. Full-size foxes use their powers of shapeshifting and illusion to hide. They must remain close at hand for when their masters need them. The pipe fox doesn't need to expend her power. These fox-sorcerers are said to be known by their strange scent. The musk of the pipe fox clings to her master. As for her name, she is called a pipe fox because she can fit into a water pipe. In fact, some rats stand taller than her. It may seem strange to keep a small fox up your sleeve. After all, large wild foxes have more power. But the pipe fox became popular around 1849 because of her ability to explain people's pasts and predict the future. Young women were fond of pipe foxes because of these abilities.[95]

The Use of Familiars

Whereas the pipe fox is useful for conversing like a dandy, full-sized wild foxes are preferred because of their shape-shifting abilities. In the story of the "Lucky Teakettle," the fox uses her shape-shifting skills to make a man rich. Fox-sorcerers gain the shape-shifting ability of the fox to use in similar ways. Within limits. Fox-sorcerers cannot be overly greedy or exploit their familiars. Otherwise, the fox will leave. Not only can a fox familiar transform graves into palaces and refuse into feasts, the fox can also mess with a rival's livestock. A wise fox-sorcerer can frame a rival to look like a fox-owner. Let's revisit Takeshi for an example.

After Takeshi was accused of being a fox-owner, his neighbor, Akira, enjoyed salting the wound. Takeshi's wealth soon decreased, and he found himself making a meager living by gathering firewood from the nearby forest. One day, Takeshi returned home to see a strange blue glow coming from his windows. His neighbors gathered and stared at the glow while Akira gloated from his window. Takeshi sagged. Everyone knew what that blue glow meant: fox.

What fox? Takeshi wished he had a fox. He wouldn't have to collect firewood if he did!

As time passed, Takeshi suffered more problems. People's things started appearing on his doorstep. He felt eyes watching him when he went for wood. Soon, few people wanted to deal with him. Oh, no one said it. They just bowed their thanks when they found some lost item by Takeshi's house, but he knew what they thought.

Using a familiar to frame a rival would be a simple matter. Simply send your familiar to pilfer things and drop them off at your rival's house like Akira does. But why frame a rival when your familiar can possess him?

Takeshi felt strange. His legs refused to listen, and his mind felt as thick as the fog coming down from Mount Inari. Why was he going to the village square? He didn't know.

The square bustled. People rushed about, preparing for the upcoming festival. Several people glanced away. Takeshi stopped and jabbed a finger at a neighbor lugging a bundle of bamboo.

"Mr. Ishi. You have been sleeping with Ms. Kyoko!" Takeshi heard his voice ring out of its own accord.

Everyone stopped and turned to him.

What am I doing? Takeshi thought. He tried to clamp his mouth shut, but his body refused to listen. His finger skewered the head council member, Mr. Yamato.

"And you. Your breath could melt iron. Everyone says so."

His finger and words stabbed at each of his neighbors, his friends. His accusing, vulgar finger passed Akira. Takeshi's heart fluttered. He understood why his body refused to listen.

What is the best method to get rid of your rival as a fox-sorcerer? Have your fox possess the man and publicly confess his deepest thoughts. A fox-familiar, particularly a high-class one, can possess someone and learn everything the victim knows. The fox can drive a rival to self-sabotage, like our poor Takeshi.

Most fox-sorcerers wanted fox familiars because of their divination, but some also wanted a fox because of their power over fire.

Fox Fire

Fox-fire, known to the Japanese as *kitsune-bi*, came with the fox on her journey from China. The Chinese fox lights these blue flames by stroking her tail. Fox-fire comes in four types: a cluster of small flames, a large fireball, an eerie blue glow, or the soft glowing lights seen during fox wedding processions.[96] Foxes marry for life to only one mate and hold weddings when the sun shines while raining.[97] Real foxes form monogamous relationships, so the idea of fox marriage is grounded in reality. We can't see the wedding procession. We can only see foxfire's soft glow. Fox-familiars sometimes marry. Being a familiar doesn't stop them from living as a fox.

Fox-fire appears in European stories as well. Known as will-o'-the-wisp, elf fire, or pixie lights, the phenomenon has a long history. In Latin, foxfire is called *ignis fatuus*, fool's fire, because of how it can lead travelers astray at night. A Japanese fox-sorcerer can use fox-fire to the same ends. Foxfire is real. Sometimes logs can glow with it, and it appears in rice paddies and swamps.[98] When certain bacteria feed off dead plant matter, they belch gases like phosphine, diphosphane, and methane. These gasses burn with little heat when exposed to oxygen. But weather conditions must be just right. The best conditions to see dancing fox-lights are at night before a storm or when it rains on a sunny, summer day.[99] In any case, a good fox-sorcerer knows how to use foxfire for his own ends.

Divination

Foxfire, shape-shifting, and possession. You'd think these abilities would entice everyone to feed a pregnant fox. Do you remember Shinano Province's pipe foxes? Their main purpose was to predict the future and help in conversations. Most people wanted to become fox-sorcerers for these abilities. Fishermen listen to fox cries to determine the weather and chances of a good catch. A personal fox would be even more useful. You could ask the fox the outcomes of a decision before you make it.

The fox's ability to see into the future extends as far back as her shape-shifting ability. The Ainu would listen to fox cries for omens, just like Japanese fisherman. However, the Ainu listened specifically for the cries of the lucky black fox. Most Ainu households possessed a fox skull used for divination.[100] In another old practice, people bury a fox up to its neck and place a plate of food just out of reach. As the fox slowly starves to death, her spirit passes to the food. A sculpture grinds the food, mixes it with clay, and fashions a fox statue for divination.[101] A kinder method involves visiting a shrine, asking a question of Inari, and leaving a plate of red beans and rice for a fox to eat. Red beans and rice are thought to be a fox favorite. If even half the plate is eaten, the omen is good.

Protection against Fox Magic

There are many ways to protect against fox-sorcery. Fox possession, as we have seen, requires more effort than breaking illusions and fox disguises. Possession requires professional exorcists and powerful invocations of Inari. Exorcism often ended with the death of the familiar. Possession puts the fox at the most risk because it is her most powerful ability.

Most ways to protect against fox magic are simple, like getting a dog. Foxes fear dogs, and dogs see through fox illusions. Other methods are just silly, like turning around and looking at someone through your legs. Seeing the fox upside down supposedly breaks her spell.[102]

Fried rat and fried tofu distract young foxes. The fox won't usually lose her transformation, but a beautiful woman or a tree eating a fried rat…well, seeing that would make you wonder. If you don't have a fried rat handy—why are you traveling Japan without one?—pinch yourself. If you don't feel anything from the pinch, you are trapped in a fox illusion. Another tip: look for an abnormally long face or a slight glow.[103]

If you are at home and hear a knock at the door, listen closely to the knock. Foxes are said to use their tails to knock on doors. The rap will sound different than a human knocking with a fist. Pinch yourself after you open the door!

Finally, eating the tongue of a fox confers protection from all her tricks. A fox tongue cannot fool another. If a fox tongue doesn't sound appetizing, keeping a seek from a ginkgo tree in a pocket offers the same protection.[104]

Western Witches and Fox-sorcerers

I'm sure some of this fox-familiar stuff reminds you of witches. Luckily, Western tradition doesn't have us eating the tongues of cats to ward off witch magic. Both Western witches and fox-sorcerers use familiars. Most of us think of a black cat when we think of witch familiars. However, European witch stories speak about a wide variety of familiars, including horses, birds, dogs, and even stags.[105] Witch familiars and foxes lend their powers and knowledge. Both transform their shapes. Witch familiars and Japanese foxes provide material wealth for their masters and predict the future.

Despite these similarities, fox-sorcerers and witches differ. Witch's familiars approach the witch-to-be first. The familiar offers its powers in return for the witch's soul.[106] The fox becomes a familiar by choice rather than through a covenant. The fox doesn't want the sorcerer's soul.

Foxes are more powerful than witch familiars—witch familiars rarely possess people. The last difference between a witch familiar and a fox favors the witch. Witch familiars can heal people; foxes cannot.

With our distance from feudal Japan, stories of fox-sorcerers are fiction. However, most people believed the stories were fact. Foxes really could become familiars, possess people, and predict the future. After the Meiji Restoration in 1868 and the rapid Westernization of Japan, fox beliefs declined. Fox stories considered to be fact became superstition. The Meiji Restoration removed power from the Tokugawa Shogunate and restored it to the Emperor of Japan. Soon afterward, Japan adopted modern technologies and restructured its political systems. Rapid modernization didn't take the fox out of Japan's soul.

Chapter 7
The Tip of the Tail

You'd think science would leave the fox behind, but Kitsune adapted. Technology gave her new ways to play her pranks: wild foxes started delivering telegrams and playing phone pranks. Thanks to these tricks, Japanese answer phones with *moshi-moshi*. The doubled phrase tests for a fox. Only old foxes speak human language well. But the word *moshi* gives even wise, old foxes trouble. An old fox can manage the word once but never twice in quick succession. Failing to answer a phone call with *moshi-moshi* is impolite and puts your humanness into question.[107] She didn't stop at phone pranks. The Japanese fox turned her shape-shifting skills toward the new creations of the modern era: trains and cars.

Late one evening, a man was walking along the narrow and steep road known as "Kurumaza-ka" ("Cart Hill"), which led down from the Inari Shrine when a huge automobile, blazing with lights, rushed up and came within a hair's breadth of hitting the pedestrian, who stepped to one side in the nick of time. Several days later, in the wee small hours of the night, this same man was in his own motor-car carefully making his way down "Kurumazaka" when again up the hill came a larger car going at tremendous speed. There was no room to pass and no time to stop. The driver in the first car put on brakes and braced himself for the collision. There was a dull thud, and the huge car disappeared. Getting out, the driver saw beneath the wheels of his car an old, dead fox![108]

Just as Japan didn't leave all of its past behind, the fox didn't leave all of her past. She appears in an old drinking game similar to rock-paper-scissors called *Kitsune-ken*. In the game, there are three different gestures. Hands at shoulder height with palms facing out represent a hunter. Two fists mimic a rifle, and hands on thighs suggest a fox running. The hunter uses the gun to kill the fox, but the fox can't use the gun against the hunter. However, the fox deceives the hunter. Three of the possible nine combinations can win.[109]

As the aristocratic classes of Japan turned away from "superstition," merchants and farmers told her stories and·played *kitsune-ken*. Even today she continues to live through popular media like manga and television. In the popular anime and manga series *Naruto*, a nine-tailed fox lives within the namesake hero. He wrestles with the fox inside him and sometimes draws upon its power. Another manga series, *Inuyasha,* features shape-shifting fox characters. The fox isn't limited to animation and comics. Director and screenwriter Akira Kurosawa sprinkles traditional fox stories into his movies. For example, the movie *Ran* tells a story about the nine-tailed fox.

The fox appears in Japanese art in her varied forms. During the Edo period, artists tried to capture her as she changed her shape. Many woodblock prints show her dressed as a human and going about human activities. Others offer glimpses of a tail peeking out from under a *kimono.*

Kitsune came from China, but she found a home in Japan. She became the shape of the Japanese soul, and her stories possess anyone who hears them. She continues to live on in Inari statues and modern stories. She still listens for us to call out: come and sleep.

Further Reading
Ainu Fox Stories

The Ainu, one of Japan's indigenous people, told stories about the fox long before Chinese fox stories crossed the Sea of Japan. Basil Hall Chamberlain collected a few of these tales in his 1886 work *Aino Folk-tales*. I selected two stories, "How a Man Got the Better of Two Foxes" and "The Two Foxes, the Mole, and the Crows," to show how the fox's pranks and shape-shifting ability changed little from Ainu tales.

How a Man Got the Better of Two Foxes

A man went into the mountains to get bark to make rope with and found a hole. To this hole, there came a fox, who spoke as follows, though he was a fox, in human language: "I know of something from which great profit may be derived. Let us go to the place to-morrow!" To which the fox inside the hole replied as follows: "What profitable thing do you allude to? After hearing about it, I will go with you if it sounds likely to be profitable; and if not, not." The fox outside spoke thus: "The profitable thing to be done is this. I will come here to-morrow about the time of the mid-day meal. You must be waiting for me then, and we will go off together. If you take the shape of a horse, and we go off together, I taking the shape of a man and riding on your back, we can go down to the shore, where dwell human beings possessed of plenty of food and all sorts of other things. As there is sure to be among the people someone who wants a horse, I will sell you to him who thus wants a horse. I can then buy a quantity of precious things and of food. Then I shall run away; and you, having the appearance of a horse, will be led out to eat grass, and be tied up somewhere on the hillside. Then, if I come and help you to escape, and we divide the food and the precious things equally between us, it will be profitable for both of us." Thus spoke the fox outside the hole; and the fox inside the hole was very glad, and said: "Come and fetch me early to-morrow, and we will go off together."

The man was hidden in the shade of the tree and had been listening. Then the fox who had been standing outside went away, and the man, too, went home for the night. But he came back next day to the mouth of the hole, and spoke thus, imitating the voice of the fox whom he had heard speaking outside the hole the day before: "Here I am. Come out at once! If you will turn into a horse, we will go down to the shore." The fox came out. It was a big fox. The man said: "I have come already turned into a man. If you turn into a horse, it will not matter even if we are seen by other people." The fox shook itself and became a large chestnut [*lit.* red] horse. Then the two went off together, and came to a very

95

rich village, plentifully provided with everything. The man said: "I will sell this horse to anybody who wants one." As the horse was a very fine one, everyone wanted to buy it. So the man bartered it for a quantity of food and precious things and then went away.

Now the horse was such a peculiarly fine one that its new owner did not like to leave it out-of-doors but always kept it in the house. He shut the door, and he shut the window and cut grass to feed it with. But though he fed it, it could not (being really a fox) eat grass at all. All it wanted to eat was fish. After about four days it was like to die. At last, it made its escape through the window and ran home, and, arriving at the place where the other fox lived, wanted to kill it. But it discovered that the trick had been played, not by its companion fox, but by the man. So both the foxes were very angry and consulted about going to find the man and kill him.

But though the two foxes had decided thus, the man came and made humble excuses, saying: "I came the other day because I had overheard you two foxes plotting, and then I cheated you. For this, I humbly beg your pardon. Even if you do kill me, it will do no good. So henceforward I will brew rice-beer for you, and set up the divine symbols for you, and worship you,—worship you forever. In this way, you will derive greater profit than you would derive from killing me. Fish, too, whenever I make a good catch, I will offer to you as an act of worship. This being so, the creatures called men shall worship you forever."

The foxes, hearing this, said: "That is capital, we think. That will do very well." Thus spake the foxes. Thus does it come about that all men, both Japanese and Aino, worship the fox. So it is said.

The Two Foxes, the Mole, and the Crows

Two brother foxes consulted together thus: "It would be fun for us to go down among men, and assume human shape." So they made treasures, and they made garments out of the leaves of various trees, and they made various things to eat and cakes out of the gum which comes out of trees. But the mole[-god] saw them making all these preparations. So the mole made a place like a human village and placed himself in it under the disguise of a very old man. The foxes came to that village; they came to the very old man's house. And the mole himself made beautiful treasures and made garments out of various herbs and leaves of trees, and, taking mulberries and grapes from the tops of the trees, he made good food. On the arrival of the foxes, the mole invited all the crows in the place and all sorts of birds. He gave them human shape and placed them as owners in the houses of the village. Then the mole, as chief of the village, was a very old man.

Then the foxes came, having assumed the shape of men. They thought the place was a human village. The old chief bought all the things which the foxes had brought on their backs, all their treasures, and all their food. Then the old man displayed to them his own beautiful treasures. The old man displayed all his beautiful things, his garments. The foxes were much pleased. Then the old man spoke thus: "Oh you strangers! As there is a dance in my village, it will be well for you to see it." Then all the people in the village danced all sorts of dances. But at last, owing to their being birds, they began to fly upwards, notwithstanding their human shape. The foxes saw this and were much amused. The foxes ate both of the mulberries and of the grapes. They tasted very good. It was great fun, too, to see the dancing. Afterward, they went home.

The foxes thought thus: "What is nicer even than treasures is the delicious food which human beings have. As we do not know what it is, let us go again and buy some more of it." So they again made treasures out of herbs. Then they again went down to that village. The mole was in a golden house—a large house. He was alone in it, having sent all the crows and the rest away. As the foxes entered the house and looked at them, they saw a very venerable god. The god spoke thus: "Oh! you foxes; because you had assumed human shape, you made all sorts of counterfeit treasures. I saw all that you did. It is by me, and because of this, that you are brought here. You think this is a human village; but it is the village of me, your master the mole. It seems you constantly do all sorts of bad things. If you do so, it is very wrong; so do not assume human shape anymore. If you will cease to assume human shape, you may henceforth eat your fill of these mulberries and grapes. You and your companions the crows may eat together of the mulberries and of all fruits at the top of the trees, which the crows cause to drop down. This will be much more profitable for you than to assume human shape." Thus spoke the mole.

Owing to this, the foxes left off assuming human shape, and, from that time forward, ate as they pleased of the mulberries and the grapes. When the crows let any drop, they went underneath the trees and ate them. They became very friendly together.

Further Reading
Chinese Fox Stories

Chinese fox stories are numerous and influential. The Japanese fox inherited most of her traits from her Chinese sisters. I selected two stories, "The Fox and the Raven" and "The Talking Silver Foxes," to illustrate the commonality of the Japanese fox's cunning and the fox's ability to speak. The stories can be found in *The Chinese Fairy Book,* edited by R. Wilhelm in 1921.

The Fox and the Raven

The fox knows how to flatter, and how to play many cunning tricks. Once upon a time he saw a raven, who alighted on a tree with a piece of meat in his beak. The fox seated himself beneath the tree, looked up at him, and began to praise him.

"Your color," he began, "is pure black. This proves to me that you possess all the wisdom of Laotzse, who knows how to shroud his learning in darkness. The manner in which you manage to feed your mother shows that your filial affection equals that which the Master Dsong had for his parents. Your voice is rough and strong. It proves that you have the courage with which King Hiang once drove his foes to flight by the mere sound of his voice. In truth, you are the king of birds!"

The raven, hearing this, was filled with joy and said: "I thank you! I thank you!"

And before he knew it, the meat fell to earth from his opened beak.

The fox caught it up, devoured it and then said, laughing: "Make note of this, my dear sir: if someone praises you without occasion, he is sure to have a reason for doing so."

The Talking Silver Foxes

The silver foxes resemble other foxes but are yellow, fire-red or white in color. They know how to influence human beings, too. There is a kind of silver fox which can learn to speak like a man in a year's time. These foxes are called "Talking Foxes."

Southwest of the bay of Kaiutschou there is a mountain by the edge of the sea, shaped like a tower, and hence known as Tower Mountain. On the mountain, there is an old temple with the image of a goddess, who is known as the Old Mother of Tower Mountain. When children fall ill in the surrounding villages, the magicians often give orders that paper figures of them be burned at her altar, or little lime images of them are placed around it. And for this reason, the altar and its surroundings are covered with hundreds of figures of children made in lime. Paper flowers, shoes, and clothing are also brought to the Old Mother and lie in a confusion of colors. The pilgrimage festivals take place on the third day of the third month and the ninth day of the ninth month, and then there are theatrical performances, and the holy writings are read. And there is also an annual fair. The girls and women of the neighborhood burn incense and pray to the goddess. Parents who have no children go there and pick out one of the little children made of lime and tie a red thread around its neck, or even secretly break off a small bit of its body, dissolve it in water, and drink it. Then they pray quietly that a child may be sent them.

Behind the temple is a great cave where, in former times, some talking foxes used to live. They would even come out and seat themselves on the point of a steep rock by the wayside. When a wanderer came by they would begin to talk to him in this fashion: "Wait a bit, neighbor; first smoke a pipe!" The traveler would look around in astonishment to see where the voice came from and would become very much frightened. If he did not happen to be exceptionally brave, he would begin to perspire with terror and run away. Then the fox would laugh: "Hi hi!"

Once a farmer was plowing on the side of the mountain. When he looked up he saw a man with a straw hat, wearing a mantle of woven grass, and carrying a pick across his shoulder coming along the way.

"Neighbor Wang," said he, "first smoke a pipeful and take a little rest! Then I will help you plow."

Then he called out "Hu!" the way farmers do when they talk to their cattle.

The farmer looked at him more closely and saw then that he was a talking fox. He waited for a favorable opportunity, and when it came, gave him a lusty blow with his ox-whip. He struck home, for the fox screamed, leaped into the air, and ran away. His straw hat, his mantle of woven grass, and the rest he left lying on the ground. Then the farmer saw that the straw hat was just woven out of potato leaves; he had cut it in two with his whip. The mantle was made of oak-leaves, tied together with little blades of grass. And the pick was only the stem of a kau-ling plant, to which a bit of brick had been fastened.

Not long after, a woman in a neighboring village became possessed. A picture of the head priest of the Taoists was hung up in her room, but the evil spirit did not depart. Since there were none who could exorcise devils in the neighborhood, and the trouble she gave was unendurable, the woman's relatives decided to send to the temple of the God of War and beg for aid.

But when the fox heard of it, he said: "I am not afraid of your Taoist high-priest nor of your God of War; the only person I fear is your neighbor Wang in the Eastern village, who once struck me cruelly with his whip."

This suited the people to a T. They sent to the Eastern village and found out who Wang was. And Wang took his ox-whip and entered the house of the possessed woman.

Then he said in a deep voice: "Where are you? Where are you? I have been on your trail for a long time. And now, at last, I have caught you!"

With that, he snapped his whip.

The fox hissed and spat and flew out of the window.

They had been telling stories about the talking fox of Tower Mountain for more than a hundred years when one fine day, a skillful archer came to that part of the country who saw a creature like a fox, with a fiery-red pelt, whose back was striped with gray. It was lying under a tree. The archer aimed and shot off its hind foot.

At once it said in a human voice: "I brought myself into this danger because of my love for sleep, but none may escape his fate! If you capture me you will get at the most no more than five thousand pieces of copper for my pelt. Why not let me go instead? I will reward you richly so that all your poverty will come to an end."

But the archer would not listen to him. He killed him, skinned him, and sold his pelt; and, sure enough, he received five thousand pieces of copper for it.

From that time on, the fox-spirit ceased to show itself.

Further Reading
Japanese Fox Stories

We've already seen a wide variety of Japanese fox stories. This chapter features several complete stories that I glossed over earlier. This collection, like the Ainu and Chinese collections, is far from exhaustive. I selected only a few stories to support our conversation with the Japanese fox. "The Foxes' Wedding" and "The Grateful Foxes" come from A.B. Mitford's *Tales of Old Japan* (1871). "The Fox and Badger," from William Giffis's *Japanese Fairy World* (1880), features the *tanuki*. The *tanuki*, also called the badger or raccoon dog, is the fox's rival. He is able to shape-shift like the fox and enjoys playing pranks. "Tamamo, The Fox Maiden" is a complete version of the "Jewel Maiden" story. It comes from Grace James's *Japanese Fairy Tales* (1910). The final story, "On a Contest Between Women of Extraordinary Strength," is a sequel to first fox-wife story "On Taking a Fox as a Wife and Bringing Forth a Child."

The Foxes' Wedding

Once upon a time there was a young white fox, whose name was Fukuyémon. When he had reached the fitting age, he shaved off his forelock and began to think of taking to himself a beautiful bride. The old fox, his father, resolved to give up his inheritance to his son and retired into private life; so the young fox, in gratitude for this, laboured hard and earnestly to increase his patrimony. Now it happened that in a famous old family of foxes there was a beautiful young lady-fox with such lovely fur that the fame of her jewel-like charms was spread far and wide. The young white fox, who had heard of this, was bent on making her his wife, and a meeting was arranged between them. There was not a fault to be found on either side; so the preliminaries were settled, and the wedding presents sent from the bridegroom to the bride's house, with congratulatory speeches from the messenger, which were duly acknowledged by the person deputed to receive the gifts; the bearers, however received the customary fee in copper cash.

When the ceremonies had been concluded, an auspicious day was chosen for the bride to go to her husband's house, and she was carried off in a solemn procession during a shower of rain, the sun shining all the while. After the ceremonies of drinking wine had been gone through, the bride changed her dress, and the wedding was concluded, without let or hindrance, amid singing and dancing and merry-making.

The bride and bridegroom lived lovingly together, and a litter of little foxes was born to them, to the great joy of the old grandsire, who treated the little cubs as tenderly as if they had been butterflies or flowers. "They're the very image of their old grandfather," said he, as proud as possible. "As for medicine, bless them, they're so healthy that they'll never need a copper coin's worth!"

As soon as they were old enough, they were carried off to the temple of Inari Sama, the patron saint of foxes, and the old grandparents prayed that they might be delivered from dogs and all the other ills to which fox flesh is the heir.

In this way, the white fox by degrees waxed old and prosperous, and his children, year by year, became more and more numerous around him, so that, happy in his family and his business, every recurring spring brought him fresh cause for joy.

The Grateful Foxes

One fine spring day, two friends went out to a moor to gather fern, attended by a boy with a bottle of wine and a box of provisions. As they were straying about, they saw at the foot of a hill a fox that had brought out its cub to play, and whilst they looked on, struck by the strangeness of the sight, three children came up from a neighboring village with baskets in their hands, on the same errand as themselves. As soon as the children saw the foxes, they picked up a bamboo stick and took the creatures stealthily in the rear. When the old foxes took to flight, the children surrounded them and beat them with the stick, and the foxes ran away as fast as their legs could carry them. But two of the boys held down the cub, and, seizing it by the scruff of the neck, went off in high glee.

The two friends were looking for all the while, and one of them, raising his voice, shouted out, "Hallo! you boys! what are you doing with that fox?"

The eldest of the boys replied, "We're going to take him home and sell him to a young man in our village. He'll buy him, and then he'll boil him in a pot and eat him."

"Well," replied the other, after considering the matter attentively, "I suppose it's all the same to you whom you sell him to. You'd better let me have him."

"Oh, but the young man from our village promised us a good round sum if we could find a fox and got us to come out to the hills and catch one, and so we can't sell him to you at any price."

"Well, I suppose it cannot be helped, then; but how much would the young man give you for the cub?"

"Oh, he'll give us three hundred cash at least."

"Then I'll give you half a bu, and so you'll gain five hundred cash by the transaction."

"Oh, we'll sell him for that, sir. How shall we hand him over to you?"

"Just tie him up here," said the other; and so he made fast the cub around the neck with the string of the napkin in which the luncheon-box was wrapped and gave half a bu to the three boys, who ran away delighted.

The man's friend, upon this, said to him, "Well, certainly you have got queer tastes. What on earth are you going to keep the fox for?"

"How very unkind of you to speak of my tastes like that. If we had not interfered just now, the fox's cub would have lost its life. If we had not seen the affair, there would have been no help for it. How could I stand by and see a life taken? It was but a little I spent—only half a bu—to save the cub, but had it cost a fortune I should not have grudged it. I thought you were intimate enough with me to know my heart, but to-day you have accused me of being eccentric, and I see how mistaken I have been in you. However, our friendship shall cease from this day forth."

And when he had said this with a great deal of firmness, the other, retiring backward and bowing with his hands on his knees, replied—

"Indeed, indeed, I am filled with admiration at the goodness of your heart. When I hear you speak thus, I feel more than ever how great is the love I bear you. I thought that you might wish to use the cub as a sort of decoy to lead the old ones to you, that you might pray them to bring prosperity and virtue to your house. When I called you eccentric just now, I was but trying your heart, because I had some suspicions of you; and now I am truly ashamed of myself."

And as he spoke, still bowing, the other replied, "Really! was that indeed your thought? Then I pray you to forgive me for my violent language."

When the two friends had thus become reconciled, they examined the cub and saw that it had a slight wound in its foot and could not walk; and while they were thinking what they should do, they spied out the herb called "Doctor's Nakasé," which was just sprouting; so they rolled up a little of it in their fingers and applied it to the part. Then they pulled out some boiled rice from their luncheon-box and offered it to the cub, but it showed no sign of wanting to eat; so they stroked it gently on the back, and petted it; and as the pain of the wound seemed to have subsided, they were admiring the properties of the herb, when, opposite to them, they saw the old foxes sitting watching them by the side of some stacks of rice straw.

"Look there! The old foxes have come back out of fear for their cub's safety. Come, we will set it free!" And with these words they untied the string around the cub's neck and turned its head towards the spot where the old foxes sat; and as the wounded foot was no longer painful, with one bound it dashed to its parents' side and licked them all over for joy, while they seemed to bow their thanks, looking towards the two friends. So, with peace in their hearts, the latter went off to another place, and, choosing a pretty spot, produced the wine bottle and ate their noon-day meal; and after a pleasant day, they returned to their homes and became firmer friends than ever.

Now the man who had rescued the fox's cub was a trades-man in good circumstances: he had three or four agents and two maid-servants, besides men-servants; and altogether he lived in a liberal manner. He was married, and this union had brought him one son, who had reached his tenth year but had been attacked by a strange disease which defied all the physician's skill and drugs.

At last, a famous physician prescribed the liver taken from a live fox, which, as he said, would certainly effect a cure. If that were not forthcoming, the most expensive medicine in the world would not restore the boy to health. When the parents heard this, they were at their wits' end. However, they told the state of the case to a man who lived on the mountains. "Even though our child should die for it," they said, "we will not ourselves deprive other creatures of their lives; but you, who live among the hills, are sure to hear when your neighbors go out fox-hunting. We don't care what price we might have to pay for a fox's liver; pray, buy one for us at any expense." So they pressed him to exert himself on their behalf; and he, having promised faithfully to execute the commission, went his way.

In the night of the following day there came a messenger, who announced himself as coming from the person who had undertaken to procure the fox's liver; so the master of the house went out to see him.

"I have come from Mr. So-and-so. Last night the fox's liver that you required fell into his hands, so he sent me to bring it to you." With these words the messenger produced a small jar, adding, "In a few days he will let you know the price."

When he had delivered his message, the master of the house was greatly pleased and said, "Indeed, I am deeply grateful for this kindness, which will save my son's life."

Then the goodwife came out and received the jar with every mark of politeness.

"We must make a present to the messenger."

"Indeed, sir, I've already been paid for my trouble."

"Well, at any rate, you must stop the night here."

"Thank you, sir: I have a relation in the next village whom I have not seen for a long while, and I will pass the night with him"; and so he took his leave, and went away.

The parents lost no time in sending to let the physician know that they had procured the fox's liver. The next day the doctor came and compounded a medicine for the patient, which at once produced a good effect, and there was no little joy in the household. As luck would have it, three days after this the man whom they had commissioned to buy the fox's liver came to the house; so the goodwife hurried out to meet him and welcome him.

"How quickly you fulfilled our wishes, and how kind of you to send at once!

The doctor prepared the medicine, and now our boy can get up and walk about the room, and it's all owing to your goodness."

"Wait a bit!" cried the guest, who did not know what to make of the joy of the two parents. "The commission with which you entrusted me about the fox's liver turned out to be a matter of impossibility, so I came to-day to make my excuses, and now I really can't understand what you are so grateful to me for."

"We are thanking you, sir," replied the master of the house, bowing with his hands on the ground, "for the fox's liver which we asked you to procure for us."

"I really am perfectly unaware of having sent you a fox's liver: there must be some mistake here. Pray, inquire carefully into the matter."

"Well, this is very strange. Four nights ago, a man of some five or six and thirty years of age came with a verbal message from you, to the effect that you had sent him with a fox's liver, which you had just procured, and said that he would come and tell us the price another day. When we asked him to spend the night here, he answered that he would lodge with a relation in the next village and went away."

The visitor was more and more lost in amazement, and, leaning his head on one side in deep thought, confessed that he could make nothing of it. As for the husband and wife, they felt quite out of countenance at having thanked a man so warmly for favors of which he denied all knowledge; and so the visitor took his leave and went home.

That night there appeared at the pillow of the master of the house a woman of about one or two and thirty years of age, who said, "I am the fox that lives at such-and-such a mountain. Last spring, when I was taking out my cub to play, it was carried off by some boys, and only saved by your goodness. The desire to requite this kindness pierced me to the quick. At last, when calamity attacked your house, I thought that I might be of use to you.

Your son's illness could not be cured without a liver taken from a live fox, so to repay your kindness I killed my cub and took out its liver; then its sire, disguising himself as a messenger, brought it to your house."

And as she spoke, the fox shed tears; and the master of the house, wishing to thank her, moved in bed, upon which his wife awoke and asked him what was the matter; but he too, to her great astonishment, was biting the pillow and weeping bitterly.

"Why are you weeping thus?" asked she.

At last, he sat up in bed, and said, "Last spring, when I was out on a pleasure excursion, I was the means of saving the life of a fox's cub, as I told you at the time. The other day I told Mr. So-and-so that, although my son was to die before my eyes, I would not be the means of killing a fox on purpose; but asked him, in case he heard of any hunter killing a fox, to buy it for me. How the foxes came to hear of this I don't know, but the foxes to whom I had shown kindness killed their own cub and took out the liver; and the old dog-fox, disguising himself as a messenger from the person to whom we had confided the commission, came here with it. His mate has just been at my pillow-side and told me all about it; hence it was that, in spite of myself, I was moved to tears."

The Fox and Badger

There is a certain mountainous district in Shikoku in which a skillful hunter had trapped or shot so many foxes and badgers that only a few were left. These were an old gray badger and a female fox with one cub. Though hard pressed by hunger, neither dared to touch a loose piece of food, lest a trap might be hidden under it. Indeed they scarcely stirred out of their holes except at night, lest the hunter's arrow should strike them. At last the two animals held a council together to decide what to do, whether to emigrate or to attempt to outwit their enemy. They thought a long while, when finally the badger having hit upon a good plan, cried out:

"I have it. Transform yourself into a man. I'll pretend to be dead. Then you can bind me up and sell me in the town. With the money paid you can buy some food. Then I'll get loose and come back. The next week I'll sell you and you can escape."

"Ha! ha! ha! *yoroshiu, yoroshiu,*" (good, good,) cried both together. "It's a capital plan," said Mrs. Fox.

So the Fox changed herself into a human form, and the badger, pretending to be dead, was tied up with straw ropes.

Slinging him over her shoulder, the fox went to town, sold the badger, and buying a lot of *tofu* (bean-cheese) and one or two chickens, made a feast. By this time the badger had got loose, for the man to whom he was sold, thinking him dead, had not watched him carefully. So scampering away to the mountains, he met the fox, who congratulated him, while both feasted merrily.

The next week the badger took human form, and going to town sold the fox, who made believe to be dead. But the badger, being an old skin-flint and very greedy, wanted all the money and food for himself. So he whispered in the man's ear to watch the fox well as she was only feigning to be dead. So the man taking up a club gave the fox a blow on the head, which finished her. The badger, buying a good dinner, ate it all himself and licked his chops, never even thinking of the fox's cub.

The cub after waiting a long time for its mother to come back suspected foul play and resolved on revenge. So going to the badger, he challenged him to a trial of skill in the art of shape-shifting.

The badger accepted right off, for he despised the cub and wished to be rid of him.

"Well what do you want to do first?" said Sir Badger.

"I propose that you go and stand on the Big Bridge leading to the city," said the cub, "and wait for my appearance. I shall come in splendid garments, and with many followers in my train. If you recognize me, you win, and I lose. If you fail, I win."

So the badger went and waited behind a tree. Soon a daimyo riding in a palanquin, with a splendid retinue of courtiers appeared, coming up the road. Thinking this was the fox-cub changed into a nobleman, although wondering at the skill of the young fox, the badger went up to the palanquin and told the person inside that he was recognized and had lost the game.

"What!" said the daimyo's followers, who were real men, and surrounding the badger, they beat him to death.

The fox-cub, who was looking on from a hill nearby, laughed in derision, and glad that treachery was punished, scampered away.

Tamamo, The Fox Maiden

A peddler journeyed with his pack upon the great high-road which leads to the city of Kyoto. He found a child sitting all alone by the wayside.

"Well, my little girl," he said, "and what make you all alone by the wayside?"

"What do you," said the child, "with a staff and a pack, and sandals outworn?"

"I am bound for Kyoto, and the Mikado's Palace, to sell my goods to the ladies of the Court."

"Ah," said the child, "take me too."

"What is your name, my little girl?"

"I have no name."

"Whence come you?"

"I come from nowhere."

"You seem to be about seven years old."

"I have no age."

"Why are you here?"

"I have been waiting for you."

"How long have you waited?"

"For more than a hundred years."

The Peddler laughed.

"Take me to Kyoto," said the child.

"You may come if you will," said the Peddler. So they went their ways together, and in time they came to Kyoto and to the

Mikado's Palace. Here the child danced in the august presence of the Son of Heaven. She was as light as the sea-bird upon a wave's crest. When she had made an end of dancing, the Mikado called her to him.

"Little maid," he said, "what guerdon shall I give you? Ask!"

"O Divinely Descended," said the child, "Son of the Gods ... I cannot ask... I am afraid."

"Ask without fear," said the Mikado.

The child murmured, "Let me stay in the bright presence of your Augustness."

"So be it," said the Mikado, and he received the child into his household. And he called her Tamamo.

Very speedily she became the mistress of every lovely art. She could sing, and she could play upon any instrument of music. She had more skill in painting than any painter in the land; she was a wonder with the needle and a wonder at the loom. The poetry that she made moved men to tears and to laughter. The many thousand characters were child's play to her, and all the hard philosophies she had at her fingers' ends. She knew Confucius well enough, the Scriptures of Buddha, and the lore of Cathay. She was called the Exquisite Perfection, the Gold Unalloyed, the Jewel without Flaw.

And the Mikado loved her.

Soon he clean forgot honor and duty and kingly state. Day and night he kept Tamamo by his side. He grew rough and fierce and passionate so that his servants feared to approach him. He grew sick, listless, and languid, he pined, and his physicians could do nothing for him.

"Alas and alack," they cried, "what ails the Divinely Descended? Of a surety, he is bewitched. Woe! woe! for he will die upon our hands."

"Out of them, everyone," cried the Mikado, "for a pack of tedious fools. As for me, I will do my own will and pleasure."

He was mad for love of Tamamo.

He took her to his Summer Palace, where he prepared a great feast in her honor. To the feast were bidden all the highest of the land, princes and lords and ladies of high estate; and, willy-nilly, to the Summer Palace they all repaired, where was the Mikado, wan and wild, and mad with love, and Tamamo by his side, attired in scarlet and cloth of gold. Radiantly fair she was, and she poured the Mikado's *saké* out of a golden flagon.

He looked into her eyes.

"Other women are feeble toys beside you," he said. "There's not a woman here that's fit to touch the end of your sleeve. O Tamamo, how I love you...."

He spoke loudly so that all could hear him and laughed bitterly when he had spoken.

"My lord ... my lord ..." said Tamamo.

Now as the high company sat and feasted, the sky became overcast with black clouds, and the moon and the stars were hidden. Suddenly a fearful wind tore through the Summer Palace and put out every torch in the great Hall of Feasting. And the rain came down in torrents. In the pitch darkness, fear and horror fell upon the assembly. The courtiers ran to and fro in a panic, the air was full of cries, the tables were overturned. The dishes and drinking vessels crashed together, the *saké* spilled and soaked into the white mats. Then a radiance was made visible. It came from the place where Tamamo was, and it streamed in long flames of fire from her body.

The Mikado cried aloud in a terrible voice, "Tamamo! Tamamo! Tamamo!" three times. And when he had done this he fell in a deathly swoon upon the ground.

And for many days he was thus, and he seemed either asleep or dead, and no one could recover him from his swoon.

Then the Wise and Holy Men of the land met together, and when they had prayed to the gods, they called to them Abé Yasu, the Diviner. They said:

"O Abé Yasu, learned in dark things, find out for us the cause, and if it may be, the cure, of our Lord's strange sickness. Perform divination for us, O Abé Yasu."

Then Abé Yasu performed divination, and he came before the Wise Men and said:

"*The wine is sweet, but the aftertaste is bitter. Set not your teeth in the golden persimmon; it is rotten at the core. Fair is the scarlet flower of the Death Lily. Pluck it not. What is beauty? What is wisdom? What is love? Be not deceived. They are threads in the fabric of illusion!*"

Then the Wise Men said, "Speak out, Abé Yasu, for your saying is dark, and we cannot understand it."

"I will do more than speak," said Abé Yasu. And he spent three days in fasting and in prayer. Then he took the sacred *Gohei* from its place in the Temple, and calling the Wise Men to him he waved the sacred *Gohei* and with it touched each one of them. And together they went to Tamamo's bower, and Abé Yasu took the sacred *Gohei* in his right hand.

Tamamo was in her bower adorning herself, and her maidens were with her.

"My lords," she said, "you come all unbidden. What would you have with me?"

"My lady Tamamo," said Abé Yasu the Diviner, "I have made a song after the fashion of the Chinese. You who are learned in poetry, I pray you hear and judge my song."

"I am in no mood for songs," she said, "with my dear lord lying sick to death."

"Nevertheless, my lady Tamamo, this song of mine you needs must hear."

"Why, then, if I must ..." she said.

Then spoke Abé Yasu:

"The wine is sweet, the aftertaste is bitter. Set not your teeth in the golden persimmon; it is rotten at the core. Fair is the scarlet flower of the Death Lily. Pluck it not. What is beauty? What is wisdom? What is love? Be not deceived. They are threads in the fabric of illusion!"

When Abé Yasu the Diviner had spoken, he came to Tamamo and he touched her with the sacred *Gohei*.

She gave a loud and terrible cry, and on the instant, her form was changed into that of a great fox having nine long tails and hair like golden wire. The fox fled from Tamamo's bower, away and away, until it reached the far plain of Nasu, and it hid beneath a great black stone that was upon that plain.

But the Mikado was immediately recovered from his sickness.

Soon, strange and terrible things were told concerning the great stone of Nasu. A stream of poisonous water flowed from under it and withered the bright flowers of the plain. All who drank of the stream died, both man and beast. Moreover, nothing could go near the stone and live. The traveler who rested in its shadow arose no more, and the birds that perched upon it fell dead in a moment. People named it the Death Stone, and thus it was called for more than a hundred years.

Then it chanced that Genyo, the High Priest, who was a holy man indeed, took his staff and his begging bowl and went upon a pilgrimage.

When he came to Nasu, the dwellers upon the plain put rice into his bowl.

"O thou Holy Man," they said, "beware the Death Stone of Nasu. Rest not in its shade."

But Genyo, the High Priest, having remained a while in thought, made answer thus:

"Know, my children, what is written in the Book of the Good Law: 'Herbs, trees, and rocks shall all enter into Nirvana.'"

With that, he took his way to the Death Stone. He burnt incense, he struck the stone with his staff, and he cried, "Come forth, Spirit of the Death Stone; come forth, I conjure thee."

Then there was a great flame of fire and a rending noise, and the Stone burst and split in sunder. From the stone and from the fire there came a woman.

She stood before the Holy Man. She said:

"*I am Tamamo, once called the Proud Perfection; I am the golden-haired Fox; I know the Sorceries of the East; I was worshiped by the Princes of Ind; I was great Cathay's undoing; I was wise and beautiful, Evil incarnate. The power of the Buddha has changed me; I have dwelt in grief for a hundred years; tears have washed away my beauty and my sin. Shrive me, Genyo, shrive me, Holy Man; let me have peace.*"

"Poor Spirit," said Genyo. "Take my staff and my priestly robe and my begging bowl and set forth upon the long journey of repentance."

Tamamo took the priestly robe and put it upon her; in one hand she took the staff, in the other the bowl. And when she had done this, she vanished forever from the sight of earthly men.

"O thou, Tathagatha," said Genyo, "and thou, Kwannon, Merciful Lady, make it possible that one day even she may attain Nirvana."

On a Contest Between Women of Extraordinary Strength

In the reign of Emperor Shoumu, there was a woman of extraordinary strength in Ogawa Market, Katakata district, Mino province. She was large, and her name was Mino no kitsune (the fourth generation of the one whose mother was Mino no kitsune). Her strength equaled that of one hundred men. Living within the marketplace of Ogawa and taking pride in her strength, she sued to rob passing merchants of their goods by force.

At that time there was another woman of great strength in the village of Katawa, Aichi district, Owari province. She was small (a granddaughter of the Venerable Doujou who once lived at Gangou-ji). As she heard that Mino no kitsune robbed passersby of their goods, she sought to challenge her by loading two hundred and fifty bushels of clams on a boat and anchoring next to the market. In addition, she prepared and loaded on a boat twenty pliable vine whips.

Kitsune came to the boat, seized all the clams, and had them sold. "Where did you come from?" she asked the owner of the clams, but she got no reply. She repeated the question but again got no answer. After Kitsune had repeated the same question four times, the owner answered, "I don't know where I came from." Kitsune, insulted, rose to hit her. Thereupon the other woman seized Kitsune's two hands and whipped her once. The whip cut the flesh. Then she used another whip which also cut the flesh. Presently ten whips had cut the flesh.

Kitsune said, "I give up! I am sorry for what I have done." The other woman, whose strength was obviously greater than Kitsune's, insisted, "From now on you shall not live in this market. If you dare do so, I will beat you to death." Completely subdued, Kitsune did not live in the market or steal again, and the people in the market rejoiced over the restoration of peace.

There has always been someone in the world with great physical power. Indeed, we know such power is attained as a result of causes in past lives.

Notes

Introduction

1   Uther, "Fox in World Literature," 134.

2   *Judges* 15:1-5.

3   Johnson, "Far Eastern Fox Lore," 35-37.

4   Griffis, "Japanese Fox Myths," 57.

5   Casal, "Goblin Fox and Badger," 1.

6   Henry, "Red Fox," 29.

7   Henry, 96.

8   Henry, 48-49.

9   Strong, 68.

10   Opler, "Rice Goddess and the Fox," 43.

11   Nozaki, *Kitsune,* 36-37.

12   Casal, 87,88.

13   Etsuko, "Interpretation of Fox Possession," 453.

14   Miyamoto, "Possessed and Possessing," 139-140.

15   De Visser, 63.

Chapter 1

16   Huntington, "Foxes and Ming-Qing Fiction," 26.

17   Tak-hung Chan, "Discourse on Fox"

18   Huntington, 136-137.

19   Kang, "Spirits, Sex, and Wealth," 28.

20   Bathgate, "Fox's Craft in Japanese Religion," 25.

21   Huntington, *Alien Kind,* 177.

22   Nozaki, *Kitsune,* 35.

23 Kawai, *Japanese Psyche,* 105.

24 Kawai, 118.

25 Huntington, "Foxes and Ming-Qing Fiction," 103.

26 Storm, "Women in Japanese Proverbs," 167-182.

27 Friedman, "Women In Japanese Society."

28 Watson, *Miraculous Events,* 14-15.

29 Nozaki, 3

30 Yamada, *World View of the Ainu,* 59.

31 Casal, "Goblin Fox and Badger," 30.

32 Bathgate, 44.

33 Campbell, *Masks of God,* 476.

34 Nozaki, *Kitsune*, viii.

35 Nozaki, 25.

36 Griffis, "Japanese Fox Myths," 57.

37 De Visser, *Fox and Badger, 67-68.*

38 Chamberlain, *Things Japanese,* 115.

39 Nozaki, 33.

40 Heine, "Wild Fox Koan," 257.

41 Hearn,*Glimpses, 165.*

42 Nozaki, 38.

Chapter 2

43 Casal, "Goblin Fox and Badger,"18.

44 De Visser, "Fox and Badger," 62.

45 Casal, 19-20.

46 Nozaki, *Kitsune,* 101-104.

47 Nozaki, 33-35.

48 *Hebrews* 13:2.

49 Casal, 18-19.

Chapter 3

50 Bathgate, *Fox's Craft,* 102-103.

51 Miyamoto, "Possessed," 140.

52 Miyamoto, 145.

53 Miyamoto, 150.

54 Chamberlain,*Things Japanese,* 119.

55 Bathgate, 131.

56 Ferejohn, *War and State Building,* 72.

57 Miyamoto, 139-140.

58 Miyamoto, 140.

59 De Visser, *Fox and Badger,* 146.

Chapter 4

60 Eguchi, "Folk Concepts," 426-428.

61 Eguchi, 423-425.

62 Yoda, *Yokai Attack,* 154.

63 Etsuko, "Interpretation of Fox Possession," 469.

64 Nozaki, *Kitsune,* 212.

65 Etsuko, 454-465.

66 Etsukol 468.

67 Egucho, 444-445.

68 Johnson, "Far Eastern Fox Lore," 47.

69 Hearn, *Glimpses.*

70   Johnson, 58.

71   Huntington, "Foxes and Ming-Qing," 104-105.

72   Bartholomew, "Strange Tales," 30.

73   Etsuko, 470.

74   Nicholas, "Mass Hysteria."

75   Nozaki, 217-218.

76   Nozaki, 18.

Chapter 5

77   Yoda, *Yokai Attack!,* 156.

78   Casal, "Inari-sama," 14-16.

79   Gubler, "Kitsune," 124.

80   Opler, 45-46.

81   Casal, 13.

82   De Visser, *Fox and Badger,* 76.

83   Gubler, 127.

84   Nozaki, *Kitsune,* 13-14.

85   Casal, "Goblin Fox and Badger," 65.

86   Casal, "Goblin Fox and Badger," 122.

87   Henry, "Red Fox."

88   Nozaki, 151-152.

89   Opler, "Rice Goddess," 45.

90   Casal, "Inari-sama," 47.

91   Griffis, "Japanese Fox Myths," 127.

92   Strong, "Most Revered," 38.

Chapter 6

93 De Visser, *Fox and Badger,* 120.

94 Johnson, , "Far Eastern Fox Lore," 59.

95 De Visser, 121-126.

96 Nozaki, *Kitsune,* 182-198.

97 Casal, "Goblin Fox and Badger,"30.

98 Rea, "Foxfire," 1.

99 Dewire, "Ghost Light," 33-35.

100 Batchelar, *Ainu,* 352.

101 De Visser, 128.

102 Opler, "Rice Goddess," 46.

103 Casal, 7-8.

104 Casal, 25.

Chapter 7

105 Murray, "Divination of Witch's Familiars," 82.

106 Wilby, "Witch's Familiars," 291.

107 Casal, "Goblin Fox and Badger," 7.

108 Buchanan, "Inari," 48-49.

109 Chamberlain, *Things Japanese,* 185.

Bibliography

1. Bartholomew, Robert, "Strange Tales from the Classroom. From Demonic Possessions to Twitching Epidemics and Itching Frenzies – The Extraordinary History of Mass Hysteria in Schools." *Skeptic Magazine 19,* no. 4 (2014):28-31.

2. Batchelor, John, "The Ainu and their Folklore," *Religion Tract Society*, (1901).

3. Bathgate, Michael, *The Fox's Craft in Japanese Religion and Folklore: Shapeshifters, Transfomers, and Duplicates.* London: Routledge, 2004.

4. Buchanan, D.C. "Inari: its Origin, Development, and Nature." *Transactions of the Asiatic Society of Japan.* 12, (1935):1-191.

5. Campbell, Joseph, *The Masks of God: Oriental Mythology.* New York: Penguin Books, 1976.

6. Casal, U.A., Inari-sama; The Japanese Rice-deity and other Crop-divinities, *Ethnos* 14, no. 4 (1949): 1-64.

7. Casal, U.A., The Goblin Fox and Badger and Other Witch Animals of Japan. *Folklore Studies.* 18 (1959): 1-93

8. Chamberlain, Basil Hall, *Aino Folk-tales,* 1886.

9. Chamberlain, Basil Hall, *Things Japanese: being notes on various subjects connected with Japan for the use of travelers and others.* London: Kelly & Walsh, 1905.

10. De Visser, M.W., "The Fox and Badger in Japanese Folklore," *Transactions of the Asiatic Society of Japan.* (1908).

11. Dewire, Elinor, "A Wee Bit o' Ghost Light," *Weatherwise* 66, no. 5 (2013): 33-39.

12. Eguchi, Shigeyuki, "Between Folk Concepts of Illness and Psychiatric Diagnosis: Kitsune-tsuki (fox possession) in a mountain village of Western Japan," *Culture, Medicine, and Psychiatry.* 15 (1991): 421-451.

13. Etsuko, Matsuoka, The Interpretation of Fox Possession: Illness as a Metaphor, *Culture, Medicine, and Psychiatry,* 15 (1991): 453-477.

14. Ferejohn, J. and Frances Rosenbluth, *War and State Building in Medieval Japan,* Standford University Press, 2010.

15. Griffis, William Elliot, *Japanese Fairy World: Stories from the Wonder-lore of Japan,* J.H. Barhyte, 1880.

16. Griffis, William, "Japanese Fox Myths," *Lippinscott's Magazine of Popular Literature and Science.* 13. (1874): 57.

17. Gubler, Greg, "Kitsune: The Remarkable Japanese Fox," *Southern Folklore Quarterly.* 38 (1974): 121-134.

18. Hearn, Lafcadio. *Glimpses of Unfamiliar Japan.* Boston: Houghton, Mifflin, 1894.

19. Heine, Steve, "Putting the 'Fox' Back in the 'Wild Fox Koan': The Intersection of Philosophical and Popular Religious Elements of the Ch'an/Zen Koan Tradition." *Harvard Journal of Asiatic Studies.* 56, no. 2 (1996): 257-317.

20. Henry, J. David, *Red Fox: The Catlike Canine,* Washington D.C.: Smithsonian Institution Press, 1996.

21. Huntington, Rania Ann, *Foxes and Ming-Qing Fiction*. Massachusetts: Harvard University, 1996.

22. Huntington, Rania, *Alien Kind: Foxes and Late Imperial Chinese Narrative*. Massachusetts: Harvard University Press.

23. James, Grace, *Japanese Fairy Tales*, 1910.

24. Johnson, T.W., "Far Eastern Fox Lore," *Asian Folklore Studies*. 33, no. 1 (1974): 35-68.

25. Kang, Xiaofei, "Spirits Sex, and Wealth: Fox Lore and Fox Worship in Late Imperial China," *What are the Animals to us? Approaches from Science, Religion, Folklore, and Art.* (2007): 22-35.

26. Kawai, Hayao, *The Japanese Psyche. Major Motifs in the Fairy Tales of Japan*. Connecticut: Spring Publications, 1996.

27. McVittie, John, "A European Glimpse of Japan in the Seventeenth Century," *The Australian Quarterly*, 21 vol 1 (1949):77-89.

28. Miller, David, Fairy Tale or Myth? *Spring* (1976): 157-164.

29. Mitford, A.B., *Tales of Old Japan*, London.,1871.

30. Miyamoto, Yuki, Possessed and Possessing: Fox-possession and Discrimination Against the Wealthy in the Modern Period of Japan. *Culture and Religion* 7, no. 2 (2006): 139-154.

31. Murray, M.A., "Divination by Witch's Familiars," *Royal Anthropological Institute of Great Britain and Ireland*, 18 (1918):81-84.

32. Nicholas, Sinclair, Mass Hysteria, *Research Starters Sociology (Online Edition)* (2009).

33. Nozaki, Kiyoshi, *Japan's Fox of Mystery, Romance, and Humor.* Tokyo:The Hokuseido Press, 1961.

34. Opler, Morris and Robert Hashima,"Rice Goddessand the Fox in Japanese Religion and Folk Practice," *American Anthropology.* 48, no. 1 (1946): 43-53.

35. Rea, John, "Fox Fire," *English Language Notes.*24 (1986):1-3.

36. Storm, Hiroko, "Women in Japanese Proverbs," *Asian Folklore Studies.* 51. (1992): 167-182.

37. Strong, Sarah, "The Most Revered of Foxes, Knowledge of Animals and Animal Power in Ainu Kamui Yakur," *Asian Ethnology.* 68, no. 1. (2009): 27-54.

38. Tak-hung Chan, Leo, *The Discourse on Foxes and Ghosts: Ji Yun and Eighteenth-Century Literati Storytelling.* Honolulu: University of Hawai-i Press, 1998. 203-4.

39. Tatar, Maria, *Off with their Heads! Fairy Tales and the Culture of Childhood.* New Jersey: Princeton University Press, 1992.

40. Uther, Han Jörg, "The Fox in World Literature: Reflections on a 'Fictional Animal,'" *Asian Folklore Studies* 65, no. 2. (2006): 133-160.

41. Watson, Burton*, Record of Miraculous Events in Japan.* New York: Columbia University Press, 2013.

42. Wilby, Emma. "The Witch's Familiars and the Fairy in Early Modern England and Scotland," *Folklore,* 111, vol 2. (2000): 283-305.

43. Wilhelm, R., *The Chinese Fairy Book,* New York: Frederick A. Stokes Company, 1921.

44. Yamada, Takako, *The World View of the Ainu: Nature and Cosmos Reading from Language.* London: Kegan Paul, 2001.

45. Yoda, Huoka and Matt Alt. *Yokai Attack! The Japanese Monster Survival Guide.* Vermont: Tuttle Publishing, 2012.

46. Zipes, Jack, *Fairy Tale as Myth. Myth as Fairy Tale.* Lexington: The University Press of Kentucky, 1994.

Christopher Kincaid enjoys studying the folklore, history, and stories from cultures around the world. When not researching about *yokai* and other aspects of Japanese culture, he works as a librarian.

Books by Christopher Kincaid
The Hunted Trilogy
> *Vixen Hunted*
> *Shepherd Hunted*
> *Memory Hunted*

Nonfiction
> *Come and Sleep: The Folklore of the Japanese Fox*
> *Tanuki: The Folklore of Japan's Trickster*
> *Under the Cherry Blossoms:*
> > *An Introduction to Japanese Tree Folklore*

You can read more about Japanese folklore, culture, and American anime culture at Christopher's blog JapanPowered.

Printed in Great Britain
by Amazon